Main Street Methodist Episcopal Church

Columbian Recipes

A Publication of the Methodist Cook-book. Edition of 1893

Main Street Methodist Episcopal Church

Columbian Recipes
A Publication of the Methodist Cook-book. Edition of 1893

ISBN/EAN: 9783744784719

Printed in Europe, USA, Canada, Australia, Japan

Cover: Foto ©Andreas Hilbeck / pixelio.de

More available books at **www.hansebooks.com**

· · · · · · THE · · · · · ·

Columbian Recipes

A PUBLICATION OF THE

Methodist Cook-Book

As Revised by the Ladies of the

Main Street M. E. Church,

AKRON, OHIO.

EDITION OF 1893.

"A good digestion to you all; and once more
I shower a welcome on you—welcome all."
—*Shakespeare.*

CAPRON & CURTICE, PROMPT PRINTERS,
AKRON, OHIO.

Index to Advertisers.

Table of Contents.

CHARLES PENNE, ARCHITECT.

MAIN STREET M. E. CHURCH.

REV. O. A. CURRY, A.M., PASTOR.

PREFACE.

DEAR FRIENDS: We extend to you a cordial greeting, and beg leave to offer you as a guide in the use of the following recipes, the advice given in the "N. Y. Christian Advocate:"

"There are two ways of using recipes. One is to follow them exactly, and the other is to vary them according to one's judgment and one's resources.

A desired recipe may call for butter in generous proportions, and one may substitute nice shortening at ten or twelve cents a pound, for butter at forty cents a pound. It may be hearsay on our part, but we never could see why nice beef fat isn't as good as butter for ordinary every-day cooking. The careful housekeeper will save and classify all her drippings (by heating them with slices of white potatoes until the latter are crisp), and keep a supply of this on hand. Sugar is cheap enough just now, but half molasses will diminish even the expense of sugar and make a very palatable cake. When eggs are very high, milk may be partially substituted; for jelly in layer cake, apples, dried or fresh, and, delicately prepared, may be used. One can't make brick without straw, and one can't make the nicest possible cake without using all that goes to the making of such a cake. The celebrated English painter, Opie, was asked what he mixed his paints with to produce such marvelous effects, and he at once replied: 'With brains, sir.' Now every recipe wants to be mixed with brains. The writer can give recipes fast enough but what she can't give is brains to mix them with. These, each experimenter must furnish herself. It is simply impossible for any woman to set a good table, various, suited to the season, and to those who sit around it, without 'giving her whole mind to it,' as Beau Brummel or Count D'Orsay did to tying his cravats. She must master the combinations of the elements under her control, and learn the secret of getting the most and best out of them. A whole library of cook books won't do this for her. What are the elements? In brief, meats, vegetables, cereals, fruits. A very cheap piece of meat may be made very delicious by skillful cooking. The very choicest vegetables may be spoiled by an ignorant cook. Bread baking is an art almost divine. Who was it called himself the Bread of life? Imagination applied to the service of the most common of fruits will produce astonishing effects. But, says the busy housewife, 'How can I give my whole mind to cooking, when there are a thousand-and-one calls on me every hour in the day?' The answer is easy as was said to the disconcerted pendulum, Jane Taylor gave an account of. For every tick, there is a second given in which to tick. The habit once formed of doing one's best in the preparation of every dish that comes on the table, combined with the exact knowledge of what that preparation should be, will in time produce the happiest results and that solves the whole question."

Seven Day Abridged Bill of Fare.

SUNDAY.

Breakfast—Oranges; oatmeal with cream; eggs on toast or mutton chops, graham gems and coffee.

Dinner—Oysters on half shell or *consomme*; stewed brisket of beef and roast chicken; brown potatoes; creamed parsnips or pickled white cabbage; celery; baked lemon pudding, fruit and coffee; ice cream.

Supper—Cold chicken and celery salad; cold raised biscuit; currant jelly; citron cake and tea.

MONDAY.

Breakfast—Fried apples and cornmeal mush; fried pork chops; egg omelet; wheat bread and coffee.

Luncheon—Veal croquettes; hot milk biscuits; baked potatoes, (sweet or Irish), sweet pickles, canned peaches; cake; tea.

Dinner—Celery or vegetable soup; roast fillet of veal with tomato sauce; mashed potatoes; boiled rice; piccalilli; cranberry or custard pie; chocolate.

TUESDAY.

Breakfast—Bananas; hominy; porter house steak; muffins; Saratoga chips; coffee.

Luncheon—Dried beef with cream; potato salad; French rolls; cup custard; olives; tea.

Dinner—Tomato soup; boiled corned beef; boiled potatoes; boiled turnips; boiled cabbage; beets boiled; cranberry pie or apple pie; coffee.

WEDNESDAY.

Breakfast—Sliced pineapple or stewed prunes; cracked wheat; fried ham and eggs or meat omelet; sour milk griddle cakes; coffee.

Luncheon—Escalloped oysters or veal stew; potato puffs; light biscuit; soft gingerbread; salmon salad; chocolate.

Dinner—Chicken cream soup or lobster soup; boiled chicken; caper sauce; escalloped onions, steamed potatoes; mixed pickles; mince pie; cocoanut pudding; wafers; coffee.

THURSDAY.

Breakfast—Strawberries or stewed apricots; graham mush or oatmeal with cream; fried pan fish; potato fillets; raised muffins; coffee.

Luncheon—Roast beef pie; fried potatoes with eggs; lettuce with cream dressing or tomato salad; buns; layer cake with banana filling; tea.

Dinner—Cream of spinach soup or mutton broth; pot roast; new potatoes *a la creme*; horse radish or catsup; string beans or corn; lemon pie; fruit; coffee.

FRIDAY.

Breakfast—Stewed peaches or blackberries; egg on toast; country sausages; baked potatoes; cream waffles; brown bread and coffee.

Luncheon—Cold beef and deviled lobster; French vegetable stew; *lyonnaise* potatoes; French rolls; cream short cake; lemonade or iced tea.

Dinner—Irish potato soup; baked pickerel or blue fish and steamed halibut; escalloped oysters or baked sweet potatoes; veal croquettes; lobster patties; custard pie; nuts, raisins and coffee.

SATURDAY.

Breakfast—Oranges or peaches and cream; fried cornmeal mush; ham and liver (calve's); sliced brown potatoes; Parker house rolls; coffee.

Luncheon—Sliced veal loaf; corn pudding; fried potatoes with eggs; soda biscuit; strawberry short cake with cream and cocoa.

Dinner—Clam or onion soup; chicken pot pie; mashed potatoes; boiled onions or parsnips; cold slaw; pickles; mince or peach pie; coffee.

THE COLUMBIAN RECIPES.

SOUPS.

Meat for soup should always be put on to cook in cold water and in a covered kettle. It ought never to boil, only simmer, in order that the essence may be thoroughly drawn out. A beef or veal shank will make excellent soup and are inexpensive. A quart of water is sufficient for a pound of meat and bone.

ASPARAGUS.—Use two bunches of asparagus, one quart of water, one quart of milk, three tablespoonfuls of butter, two of flour, one onion, enough salt and pepper to season lightly. Cook the asparagus for thirty minutes in the water. Slice the onion very thin and fry from six to ten minutes in the melted butter and be very careful not to burn; then add to the asparagus and stir constantly for five minutes; then add the flour and cook for twenty minutes longer, rub through a sieve and add the milk which has just been brought to a boil. Season with salt and pepper.

BEAN.—Soak one quart of beans over night. Next day simmer together two and one-half pounds of beef and one-half pound of bacon, cut into small pieces, for two and one-half hours in about five quarts of water. When it has come to a boil remove from the fire and strain; then add the beans with one quart more of water and a dessert spoonful of powdered celery seed, then boil until the meat falls into shreds, and the beans are thoroughly dissolved. Drop into it small squares of toast and serve hot.

BEAN.—Soak a pint of beans for six hours, in three quarts of cold (soft) water. Then pour off this water and add three quarts of fresh water. Boil gently four hours, then season with an eighth of a pound of butter, two tablespoonfuls of nice lard or beef droppings, four cloves, a

Our Workmen the Best.

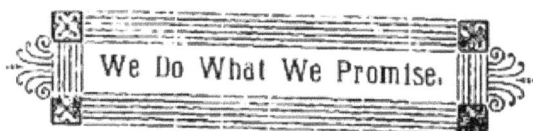

few whole allspice, a piece of celery, an onion, half of a carrot (both grated) and a tablespoonful of browned flour. Cut two hard-boiled eggs into a tureen, in which is a thinly sliced lemon, pour the soup over and serve.

CHICKEN.—An old chicken is always best for soup. Quarter the chicken and if nice and fat add a quart of water for each pound; bring slowly to a gentle boil and continue until the meat drops from the bones, then add half a cup of rice, which has been boiled previously, and a little parsley and also a half tablespoonful of flour, salt and pepper to taste.

CORN.—Cut and scrape one dozen ears of sweet corn; boil in one quart of water until well done; add two quarts of sweet milk, bring to a boil, add a quarter of a pound of butter rubbed into two tablespoonfuls of flour; season with salt and pepper. Pour the boiling soup over the yolks of two eggs well beaten, stirring all the time. Serve.

DUCHESS.—Fry two large onions in two tablespoonfuls of butter for about eight minutes, then stir in one tablespoonful of flour and let cook two minutes (be careful not to burn). Stir this into three pints of boiling milk, add two well-beaten eggs, season with salt and pepper and if desired add two tablespoonfuls of grated cheese.

EGG.—Beat an egg in a bowl, add salt, a little chopped parsley and a small teaspoonful of boiling water. Break into it toasted bread and pour the soup over it.

MRS. GEO. W. PLUMER.

NOODLE.—Into about two quarts of soup broth of any kind drop noodles made as follows: One egg, a little salt, two tablespoonfuls of milk (sweet) or water and flour enough to make a stiff dough. Roll as thin as a wafer, dredge lightly with flour, roll tightly and cut from the end as fine as possible with a sharp knife.

"SWISS WHITE."—A sufficient quantity of broth for six persons; boil it; beat well three eggs, two spoonfuls of flour, one cup of milk; pour these gradually through a sieve into the boiling soup. Add salt and pepper.

WHITE HOUSE.

CAPITAL, $100,000.00.

THE

People's Savings Bank,

Does a General Banking Business.

706 South Main Street, AKRON, O.

The accounts of individuals, business firms and corporations received subject to check. Personal and family accounts especially invited.

Interest at four per cent. per annum will be paid on Savings Deposits from date of deposit to date of withdrawal, on all amounts remaining thirty days, or longer, and any sum from One Dollar up, will be received.

Guardians, executors and private individuals holding funds awaiting investment, will find it convenient to let them lie with us, drawing INTEREST until deciding upon what securities to buy or investments to make.

Ladies will find this a particularly desirable place to do their banking. All facilities and accommodations will be furnished them, and any information regarding financial matters cheerfully given.

We will transact carefully and confidentially any and all business entrusted to our care, and give personal attention to the wants of our depositors.

Inviting you to call and inspect our office, we are

Respectfully,

THE PEOPLE'S SAVINGS BANK CO.

TOMATO.—Stew about three pints of peeled tomatoes until soft, strain and set over the fire again and add a quart of boiling milk; season with salt, pepper a good sized piece of butter, three tablespoonfuls of rolled crackers, serve hot. Canned tomatoes may be used the same way.

VEGETABLE.—Three and one-half pounds of rib beef, (not lean) wash and place in a kettle with three quarts of water, and a very little salt; let it boil gently for about four hours; then lift out the meat and strain the soup; set back on the fire and add three good-sized potatoes, two parsnips, two turnips, one onion and a little cabbage and one carrot, all of which have been cut into small pieces. Boil until the vegetables are well done.   MRS. T. J. SMITH.

FISH.

BAKED WHITE.—Clean the fish and rub salt over it; make a stuffing as for fowls, of bread crumbs, seasoned with salt and pepper, and a little sage. Fill the fish and tie it up; tie a paper over the end and bake like meat. Any large fish may be used instead of white fish.

BREAKFAST.—Pick salt codfish into small bits, and soak over night in water. Into a saucepan put milk, and a small lump of butter; when hot, squeeze the fish from the water, and put into it; and the moment it comes to a boil thicken with flour dissolved in a little cold milk, or an egg stirred in briskly.

BROILED.—Dress, wash and cut in convenient pieces; place on a broiler over coals; turning occasionally till done. Do not have as hot a fire as for steak. This is a good way to cook fish for persons with delicate stomachs, and is especially desirable where the fish is apt to be fat like the white fish.

CANNED SALMON.—This is nice either cold or warm. Heat it by placing the can in a dish of boiling water for a short time. Pour into a dish, and serve plain, or with any kind of fish sauce.   MRS. E. W. GAYLORD.

FISH CHOWDER.—Take haddock or bass and cut in pieces two or three inches square and an inch thick. Put a few slices of salt pork in an iron pot and fry till crisp; remove the pieces, chop them fine, and put in the pot a layer of fish, then a layer of split crackers and potatoes, then another layer of fish, and so on till all is used. Mix in the chopped pork with pepper and chopped onions, pour over it boiling water, cover closely and stew slowly till the fish is done. Serve with the gravy thickened with flour, or milk alone.

DRAWN BUTTER.—Rub one tablespoonful of flour with a quarter of a pound of butter; when well mixed, put in a saucepan with a tablespoonful of milk or water. Set in a dish of boiling water, shaking it well until the butter melts and is near boiling. Do not put it directly on the stove; as the heat will make the butter oil and spoil it. Vary it by adding cream, hard boiled eggs, or lemon juice; and if you desire to use it for meats, the different herbs cut fine and thrown into boiling water before adding are nice.

STANDARD.

BAKED CODFISH.—Soak the fish over night; in the morning put it to cook in water enough to cover. When tender, pick very fine, and to each pint of fish add a tablespoonful of butter, two beaten eggs, one-half teaspoonful of pepper, and 1½ pints of mashed potatoes. Mix well together, bake in a pudding dish to a delicate brown. Make a sauce of drawn butter, into which cut up a hard-boiled egg.

CODFISH DINNER.—Three pints of mashed potatoes, ½ pound or 1 package of the prepared shredded cod-fish, mix together as for fish balls and season, keep hot—boil six eggs hard and chop fine—mix half cup of butter with large spoon of flour, into this pour 1½ pints boiling water, let boil till flour is cooked then add the chopped eggs—serve both dishes hot—excellent. MRS. H. W. BENNETT.

BAKED HALIBUT.—Take a nice piece of Halibut weighing three or four pounds, and lay it in salt water 1 hour, wipe dry and score outer skin; set it in a dripping pan in a moderately hot oven and bake half an hour, basting after with water and butter heated together, when a fork penetrates

in easily, it is done; it should be a fine brown color; take the gravy in the dripping pan, and add a little boiling water, stir in a tablespoonful of catsup, the juice of half a lemon; thicken with browned flour, boil up once and put in a sauce boat.—[White House.

BOILED SALT MACKEREL.—Wash and clean off all the brine and salt; put it to soak with the meat side down, in cold water over night; in the morning rinse in one or two waters; wrap each up in a cloth and put it into a kettle with considerable water, which should be cold and cook thirty minutes; take it carefully from the cloth; take out the back bones and pour over it a little melted butter and cream, add a light sprinkle of pepper, or make a cream sauce like the following: Heat into it a teaspoonful of corn starch, wet with a little water. When this thickens add two tablespoonfuls of butter. Beat an egg light, pour the sauce gradually over it, put the mixture again over the fire and stir one minute, pour upon the fish and serve it with some slices of lemon; use parsley or water cresses to garnish the dish.—[White House.

FRIED SALT MACKEREL.—Select as many salt mackerel as possible, wash and cleanse them well, then put them to soak all day in water, changing the water every two hours; then put them into fresh water just before retiring. In the morning drain off the water, wipe them dry, roll them in flour, fry in a little butter, on a hot thick-bottom frying pan. Serve with a little melted butter poured over them.—[White House.

STEWED CODFISH.—Take a white piece of salt codfish and lay it in cold water for a few minutes; shred it; put it over the fire with cold water, let it come to a boil, and turn the water off carefully and add a pint of milk to the fish or more according to quantity. Set it over the fire again and let it boil slowly three minutes, then add a good sized piece of butter, shake of pepper, and thickening of a tablespoonful of flour, in enough cold milk to make a cream; stew five minutes longer and just before serving stir in two well-beaten eggs if desired.—[White House.

SALMON LOAF.—Remove skins, bones, etc., from one small can of salmon. Chop fish fine and rub in one tablespoonful of melted butter (not hot), mix well; beat four eggs lightly and add to them ½ cup of fine bread crumbs with pepper and salt; add to fish; put in buttered mold and steam one hour.

SAUCE FOR SALMON LOAF.—One cup boiling milk, thicken with one tablespoonful of cornstarch and one tablespoonful of butter rubbed well together; add the liquor of the salmon left in the can; add one raw egg beaten light, little pepper, put egg in last. Carefully pour over loaf. Serve.

MRS. HENRY PERKINS.

OYSTERS.

ESCALLOPED.—Take rolled crackers or fine bread crumbs and cover the bottom of a well-buttered-pan, then add a layer of oysters, seasoned with salt and pepper, and plenty of butter; another of crumbs, and so on until the dish is full, finishing with crumbs and bits of butter. Pour over it the oyster liquor, with water and milk added; cover and bake about half an hour. Some prefer to wet each layer of crumbs with the milk. MRS. G. D. BATES.

FRIED.—Drain carefully, sprinkle with pepper and salt, and set in a cool place for a few minutes. Roll in beaten egg, then in cracker crumbs, make into balls with the hand, and fry in hot lard like doughnuts. MRS. B. C. HERRICK.

CROQUETTES.—Scald and chop fine the hard part of the oysters, add an equal weight of mashed potato; to one pound of this add a piece of butter the size of an egg. teaspoonful of salt, half teaspoonful of pepper, and a quarter of a teacup of cream. Make in cakes and fry the same as in above recipe for fried oysters.

OYSTER PIE.—Line a deep pie plate with paste, dredge with flour, put in one pint of oysters, season with salt, pepper and butter. Add some of the liquor, sprinkle with flour and cover with pie crust, leaving an opening for the steam to escape.

OYSTER STEW.—Place the oysters with their liquor in a saucepan, and let them just come to a boil. Skim well. Have ready milk heated boiling hot, in the proportion of a quart of milk to a quart of oysters ; pour over the oysters, season and serve hot. If the crackers are not new they can be crisped and freshened by heating in the oven.

PICKLED OYSTERS.—Put the oysters on to scald with considerable salt. After they have just boiled up, skim them into an earthen vessel of some kind. Pour half the broth away, then take one-half pint of vinegar, a few whole cloves, same of whole pepper; put them into the broth in the kettle and bring to a boil; pour over the oysters and let stand until you want to use them.   MRS. G. D. BATES.

OYSTER SALAD.—Drain the liquor from a quart of fresh oysters—put them in hot vinegar enough to cover them—place over the fire; let them remain until "plump" but not cooked. Then drop them immediately into cold water; drain off, and mix with them two pickled cucumbers cut fine, also a quart of celery cut in dice pieces—season with salt and pepper. Mix all well together—tossing up with silver fork, pour over the whole a "Mayonaise dressing", garnish with celery tips and slices of hard boiled eggs.
MRS. HENRY PERKINS.

OYSTER SOUP.—For a quart of oysters, put a quart of milk to boil, and add to it a good lump of butter. Pour the liquid from the oysters into the hot milk, add pepper and salt and finely rolled crackers to thicken. About five minutes before serving, put in the oysters.

OYSTER PIE.—Stew enough oysters to make a pie the size you wish. If the liquor is fresh, stew the oysters in it—that is, let them just come to a boil. Season with salt and pepper, and mix together two tablespoonfuls of corn starch or flour with two tablespoonfuls of butter to a pint of the stew; line a deep earthen pie plate with a rich paste a quarter of an inch thick, then put in the oysters and cover with an upper crust, solid, or with strips of paste laid across; then bake.

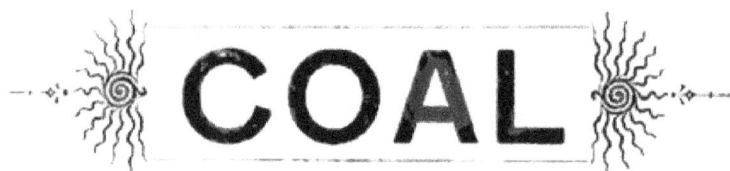

OYSTER CHOWDER.—Put thin slices of salt pork into bottom of a kettle, then a layer of thin sliced potatoes, then oysters over the potatoes, season with salt and pepper, add some butter; pour over each layer half a tea cup of tomato catsup, put in as many layers as you may wish; pour over the whole of the liquor of the oysters, cover tightly, and let stew slowly for half an hour.

CREAM OYSTERS.—One pint of cream, a little more than a pint of oysters, one tablespoonful of flour; salt and pepper to taste. Let the cream come to a boil. Mix the flour with a little cold milk and stir into the boiling cream. Let the oysters come to a boil in their own liquor, then skim carefully, drain off all the liquor, and turn the oysters into the cream.

RAW.—Drain them well in a colander, sprinkle over plenty of pepper and salt, and let them remain in a cold place for at least half an hour before serving. This makes a great difference in their flavor. They may be served in the half shell, with quarters or halves of lemon on the same dish. A very pretty arrangement is to serve them in a block of ice. Select a ten-pound block; melt with a hot flat-iron a symmetrically-shaped cavity in the top to hold the oysters. Chip also from the sides at the base, so that the ice block may stand in a large platter on a napkin. When the oysters are well salted and peppered, place them in the ice, and let them remain in the same place where the ice will not melt until the time of serving. The salt will help to make the oysters very cold. The ice may be decorated with leaves or smilax vines, and a row of lemon quarters or halves may be placed around the platter at the base of the ice. This mode of serving is very effective by gas-light.

ESCALLOPED OYSTERS IN SHELLS.—These may be served cooked in their shells or in silver scallop shells, when they present a better appearance than when cooked and served all in one dish. If cooked in an oyster or clam shell, one large or two or three small oysters are placed in it, with a few drops of the oyster liquor. It is sprinkled with pepper and salt, and cracker or bread crumbs and little pieces of butter are placed over the top. When all are ready, they

are put in the oven. When plump and fat they are done.
Brown the top with a salamander or a red-hot kitchen
shovel.

If they are cooked in the silver scallop shells, which are
larger, several oysters are served in one shell. One or two
are put in, peppered, salted, strewed with cracker crumbs
and small pieces of butter, then more layers, until the shell
is full, or until enough are used for one person. Moisten
with oyster juice and strew little pieces of butter over the
top. They are kept in the oven until thoroughly hot, then
browned with a salamander. Serve one shell on a small
plate for each person at the table.

OYSTER FRITTERS.—Drain and wipe dry as many oysters as you want to use. Beat six eggs very light, and stir
into them six tablespoonfuls of flour and one-and-a-half
pints of rich milk; beat all to a smooth batter. Have in a
pan on the stove some butter and lard; when it begins to
froth put a small ladle full of the batter, with an oyster in
the middle, into it to fry. If too thin, add flour; if too thick,
milk

OYSTER FRITTERS.—Drain as many oysters as you may
want to use; sprinkle salt and pepper over them. Make a
batter of three well beaten eggs, four tablespoonfuls of
milk and enough flour to make a thin batter. Heat enough
lard to swim the fritters in. Have two large spoons; put a
little batter into one spoon, then an oyster and drop on it
more batter from the other spoon, then drop it into the hot
lard and fry quickly without burning.

FRICASSEE OF OYSTERS.—Put one quart, or 25 oysters
on the fire in their own liquor; the moment they begin to
boil turn them into a hot dish through a colander, leaving
the oysters in the colander. Put into the saucepan two
ounces of butter (size of an egg), and when it bubbles
sprinkle in one ounce (a tablespoonful) of sifted flour; let it
cook a minute without taking color, stirring it well with an
egg-whisk, then add, mixing well, a cupful of oyster liquor.
Take from the fire, and mix in the yolks of two eggs, a little
salt, a little cayenne pepper, one teaspoonful of lemon
juice and nutmeg; beat well, then return to the fire to set the
eggs without boiling, then put in the oysters.

OYSTER PATES.--In puffs of rich pastry, put two or three oysters stewed in a dressing of cream; cover a round of the pastry and serve. Both puffs and oysters must be hot.

To ROAST OYSTERS.--Wash and wipe one peck large shell oysters; put in a hot oven, taking care to put the upper shell downward so the juice will not escape. As soon as the shells open, lay on a hot dish and serve with horse-radish or pepper-sauce, after sprinkling on them a little salt and putting a bit of fresh butter on each oyster.

STEAMED.--Wash shell oysters perfectly clean, lay them on a steamer, the upper shells down so the juice will not escape from the shells when opened. Cover the lid of the steamer with a coarse towel and press closely on. Set this over a pot of water boiling hard. In from twenty minutes to half an hour the shells will have opened. Have ready a deep plate hot, on which lay the oysters. Sprinkle salt, pepper and a bit of fresh butter on each oyster; serve immediately.

POULTRY.

CHICKEN PIE.--Two quarts of flour, work into it one tablespoonful of salt and three teaspoonfuls of baking powder, one teacup of lard worked in next, one coffee cup of cream and about as much water mixed thoroughly together to prevent streaking; if the cream is sour, sweeten it with soda. The crust will cover a six-quart pan. Bake without a bottom crust. Roll a thin crust and place about the sides of the pan, put in the chicken which has been thoroughly stewed, and season with pepper and salt. Roll the remainder of the crust round, cut a large opening in the center, and watch that it does not close in baking. After the cover is on and sealed by pressing the thumb around the edges, put a funnel in the opening, and pour in a quart of chicken broth. Make the rest of the broth into gravy to serve with the pie. Some think it a great addition to pour a pint of stewed and seasoned sweet corn over the chicken, (canned

Caswell & Alderfer,

⟨⟩ The Caterers ⟨⟩

DESIRE to say to our many friends and patrons that we have a full line of Fine China, Silver, Linen, Tables and Chairs for serving Balls, Parties, Receptions, Dinners and Teas.

Eat Candy, but eat it PURE. PURE Confections is our Motto. Bon-Bons, Chocolates and Caramels. Ice Cream Soda made of Pure Fruit JUICES and SPRING WATER. Side Drinks, Ginger Ale, Congress and Deep Rock Mineral Water. Hosford's Acid of Phosphate Soda.

SPECIAL PRICES to Churches and Societies on ICE CREAM.

Ices and Sherbets, Tutti Frutti and all Fruit Creams in Season.

. . . . . WE ARE AGENTS FOR . . . . .

WORLD'S FAIR GUMS,
      JONES' COLUMBIAN FRUIT,
           JONES' PEPSIN PHOSPHATE,
                JONES' TUXEDO GUM.

Ask your Grocer and Druggist for them. Our Telephone, 260. Orders by mail promptly attended to. Home-made Cakes made to order.

FREE DELIVERY.   **175 S. Howard St., Akron, O.**

corn will do) just before putting on the crust. It will take about two hours in a good oven to bake it. As it is not always possible to get rich cream, I will add another recipe for crust, which, although not so desirable, is still very acceptable: Two quarts of flour, six tablespoonsful of lard slighly heaped, three and a quarter cups of water or milk, two teaspoonfuls of soda stirred in the milk, four teaspoonfuls of cream tartar sifted into the dry flour and one teaspoonful of salt. Work up lightly and quickly, and do not get it too stiff. MRS. G. C. BERRY.

CHICKEN POT PIE.—Cut up a chicken, put in hot water enough to cover, and do not let it boil dry. When nearly done add pared potatoes, and dumplings made as you do biscuits. Boil or steam the dumplings; if the former, do not put them in until the potatoes are boiling, and then do not lift the cover until they are done, about half an hour. Dish potatoes by themselves, and chicken and dumplings together.

ESCALLOPED CHICKEN.—Boil two large chickens with a piece of pork, cut them in small pieces and season to your taste with salt, pepper and butter. Chop fine one pint of oysters, mix with the chicken and prepare the same as escalloped oysters. MRS. G. D. BATES.

FRICASSEED CHICKEN.—Cut up the chicken and put in a saucepan with barely enough water to cover. Stew gently till tender, then drain and fry with a few slices of salt pork till a nice brown. Take out the pork and chicken, pour in the broth, thicken with flour smoothed in a little milk, and pour over the chicken which has been kept hot.

PRESSED CHICKEN.—Take one or two chickens, boil in small quantity of salt, and when thoroughly done take all the meat from the bones, removing the skin and keeping the light meat separate from the dark; chop and season to taste with salt and pepper. If a meat presser is at hand take it, or any other mold such as a crock or pan will do put in a layer of light and a layer of dark meat till all is used. Add the liquor it was boiled in, which sould be about one teacupful and put on a heavy weight. When cold cut in

KIND FRIENDS!

Don't Read the contents of this page unless you

want to progress with the age. · · · · · · · · · ·

We try to give you goods of sterling worth, and if we fail, none
can be found upon the earth.

Sauder's Cough Syrup is warranted to cure or money refunded.
It is pleasant to take and very effective. Ask for SAUDER'S COUGH
SYRUP and take no other, for if it does not relieve you, your druggist
or grocer will refund your money. Price, 25 cents.

Sauder's Cholera Balm is a sure preventative and cure for all
Stomach and Bowel Troubles. No family should be without it, as a
dose or two taken in time will prevent serious troubles and many a
doctor's bill. Take our advice and get a bottle; you will never regret
it. Price, 25 cents.

Sauder's Golden Oil is a Liniment not surpassed by any in the
market for all purposes where an external remedy is required. For
Sore Throat, Rheumatism, Headache, etc., it cannot be equalled.
Price, 25 cents.

Sauder's Fragratine, as hundreds testify every day, is the most
delightful preparation ever make for Burns, Chapped Hands and Face,
and all Roughness of the Skin from any cause. Ladies find it invalu-
able in keeping their hands soft and smooth as silk; it is easily applied
and is not greasy or sticky. Just try one bottle. Price, 15 cents.

**Sauder's Liver and Headache Pills. Sauder's Corn and
Wart Cure, Dental Toothache Remedy** and all other of our
preparations you will find to be, and do, all we claim for them, and if
you will once give them a trial, you will find we are telling you nothing but what has been proven in thousands of cases.

There has been very much dissatisfaction the past few years, on
account of the adulteration of food products. Flavoring Extracts are
adulterated more than anything else in the grocer's stock, when it is
one of the most essential things that they should be pure. Our greatest
aim has been to produce extracts pure and unadulterated, and know
they will stand the test of any analysis. We have not only aimed at
purity, but also at cheapness, and are confident our Extracts are as
cheap and much cheaper than much of the poisonous trash sold as
Lemon and Vanilla. When using the recipes contained in this book
you will always meet with good results by using SAUDER'S EX-
TRACTS.

· · · · MANUFACTURED BY · · · ·

R. SAUDER & CO.,

AKRON, OHIO.

slices. Many chop all the meat together, add one pounded cracker to the liquor it was boiled in, and mix all thoroughly before putting in the mold.—Buckeye Cookery.

CHICKEN CROQUETTES.—Boil the chicken and take the meat (without any skin) and chop fine. season with butter, pepper, salt, cream and a little nutmeg. Dip it in egg that is well beaten, cover with rolled crackers, in which is a little pepper and salt. Make into small patties and fry brown.

MRS. D. L. KING.

ROAST TURKEY.—Dress the turkey and stuff it with a dressing of fine bread crumbs seasoned with pepper, salt and butter. A few oysters are quite an addition, and some like a little sage also. The following is abridged from "Buckeye Cookery": Place in an oven not quite as hot as for roasting meats; put a tablespoonful of butter in bits on the breast, baste often, watching and turning it occasionally to expose all parts alike to the heat. It should be moist and tender, not in the least blistered or shriveled, till a golden brown all over. For the first two-thirds of the time allowed for cooking (twenty minutes to the pound and twenty minutes longer) the surface should not crisp at all. When half done season with two teaspoonfuls of salt. In the last third of the time allowed for cooking, withdraw the pan partly from the oven, and dredge the breast, upper portion and sides thoroughly, by sifting flour over it with a fine sifter; return the pan to the oven and let remain till the flour is well browned, then baste freely with drippings from the pan and flour again; repeating this process three or four times, the crust growing crisper each time. Do not wash off the flour by basting; give it time to brown on thoroughly, and do not remove from the oven till the last dredging of flour is well browned. If necessary to turn the turkey in the pan, use a towel, not a fork. To make the gravy, boil the liver, gizzard and neck in two quarts of water for two hours, chop gizzard, heart and liver, put back and thicken with one tablespoonful of flour wet with cold water. Season with salt and pepper, and after the turkey has been taken up, pour into the dripping pan, set on top of the stove, and boil five minutes; stirring constantly, and scraping the rich particles from the sides of the pan. Serve in a gravy boat.

CHICKEN RISSOLES.--Take cold baked chicken left from dinner. Free the meat from the bones and chop fine. Rub a little dried bread into fine crumbs and to this add any heated liquor of chicken or hot water and moisten the bread thoroughly. To a pint bowl of crumbs and meat allow one teaspoonful of salt, one of pepper, one of sifted sage and one heaping teaspoonful of butter. Make into little cakes, dust with flour and fry to a light brown.

MRS. H. PERKINS.

CHICKEN PIE.—For a dish holding three quarts, use two chickens weighing about eight pounds, sufficient quantity of paste, three pints of chicken stock, four tablespoonfuls of butter, four of flour, two slices of carrot, half a large onion, a bay leaf, a sprig of parsley, a bit of mace, and salt and pepper to suit the taste—perhaps half a teaspoonful of pepper and three teaspoonfuls of salt. After cleaning and halving the chickens, put them into a kettle, cover them with boiling water, and place them where they will simmer until tender. If they are a year old, they will need to be cooked for an hour and a half. Let them cool in the water; then free them of skin, and cut into pieces suitable for serving. Put these pieces into the pie dish, sprinkle each layer with salt and pepper, about half the pepper and two teaspoonfuls of salt being used. Now put the butter into a saucepan, and beat it until soft. Add the flour, and beat until the mixture is light and creamy. Next add the vegetables, spice and herbs, besides three pints of the water in which the chickens were boiled. Heat slowly to the boiling point, and set back where the mixture will simmer for 15 minutes. Add the remaining pepper and a teaspoonful of salt, then strain the sauce over the meat. Roll out the paste, having it little larger than the top of the dish. Cut it with a knife in the center, that steam may escape, and place it over the chicken, turning the edge into the dish. Bake in a moderate oven for an hour and a quarter. It gives the pile rather a more festive appearance if the paste trimmings be rolled thin, cut in ornamental shapes, and disposed on the cover of the pie before baking.

FRIED CHICKEN.—Wash and cut up a young chicken; wipe it dry; season with salt and pepper, dredge with flour,

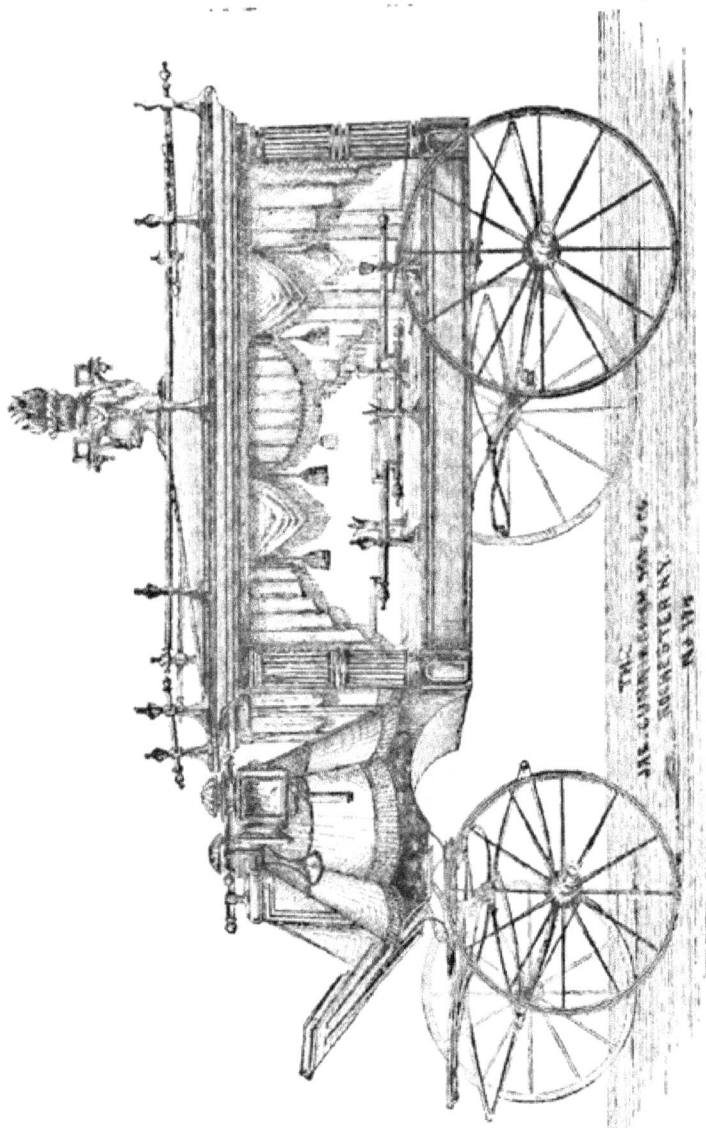

GEORGE BÜLOW,

FUNERAL DIRECTOR,

Office, Cor. Howard and Mill Sts.
Warerooms, No. 110 Ash St.

AKRON, OHIO.

Telephone 71. Open at All Hours.

or, dip each piece in beaten egg and then in crackers; have in a frying pan one ounce each of butter and sweet lard, made boiling hot; lay in the chicken, and fry brown on both sides; take up, drain them, and set aside in a covered dish; stir into the gravy left a large tablespoonful of flour; make it smooth, add a cup of milk; season with salt and pepper; let it boil and pour over the chicken. If the chicken is old put into a stew pan with a little water, and simmer gently till tender; season with salt and pepper; dip in flour or cracker crumbs and eggs and fry as above.

ROAST DUCK (TAME).—Pick, draw, clean thoroughly, and wipe dry, put the neck close to the back, beat the breast bone flat with a rolling pin, tie the wings and legs securely and stuff with the following: Three pints bread crumbs, six oz. butter, or part butter and salt pork, two chopped onions and salt. Do not stuff very full and sew up the openings firmly to keep the flavor in and the fat out. If not fat enough it should be larded with salt pork, or tie a slice upon the breast. Place in a baking pan with a little water, and baste frequently with salt and water; some add onion and some vinegar, turn often, so that the sides and back may be nicely browned. When nearly done baste with butter and a little flour. Young ducks should roast from twenty-five to thirty minutes, and full-grown ones for an hour or more, with frequent basting. Some prefer them underdone and served very hot; but, as a rule, thorough cooking will prove more palatable. Make a gravy out of the neck and gizzards by putting them in a quart of cold water, that must be reduced to a pint by boiling. The giblets, when done, may be chopped fine and added to the juice. Serve with jelly or any tart sauce.—White House.

MOCK DUCK.—Take the round of beef steak, salt and pepper either side, prepare bread or crackers with oysters or without, just as you would for stuffing a turkey, lay your stuffing on the meat, sew up and roast about an hour. Make a sauce or gravy with the drippings in the pan in which the meat is roasted, thicken the gravy with flour, moistened with water. Serve on platter, garnished with parsley or celery.
MRS. F. H. MASON.

The Great Columbian Remedy.

OVER 250 DOSES FOR ONE DOLLAR.

THE BEST and cheapest remedy on the market. Three kinds of medicine in each box. The first acts on the Stomach, Liver and Kidneys. The second is a Blood Purifier, Tonic and Nervine. The third is a Blood Enricher and Blood Maker. Put up in the form of compressed tablets, easy to take, and are guaranteed by a Bank Draft, to cure Malaria, Biliousness, Chills and Fever, Fainting, Pain in the Side, Back or Limbs, Sour Stomach, Flatulence, Dizziness, Headache, Constipation, Indigestion, and all Diseases of the Stomach, Kidneys, Liver, Bowels and Bladder. After taking a box of The Columbian Remedy if not satisfied with the result, return the empty box and get your money.

WE ATTACH A FEW OF THE HUNDREDS OF TESTIMONIALS WHICH WE HAVE RECEIVED.

BEST I EVER SAW.

AKRON, O., December 2d, 1892.

GENTLEMEN:—I have been taking Columbian Remedy and believe it is the best blood purifier and enricher I ever saw; know a good many who are or have been taking it, and they all pronounce it the best medicine they ever used.   W. S. EGAN.

CAN CHEERFULLY RECOMMEND IT.

Columbian Medicine Company: AKRON, O., December 1st, 1892.

GENTLEMEN: Have been taking Columbian for stomach trouble, indigestion, etc., and it has done me more good than anything I ever took and can cheerfully recommend it.   Yours truly,   GEORGE SEAR.

HAS NO EQUAL.

Columbian Medicine Company: AKRON, O., December 7th, 1892.

GENTLEMEN:—I procured from your agent, J. W. Hudson, a box of Columbian remedy, which for stomach trouble, I think has no equal. After several doses my stomach and head were in better condition than for a long time. I was troubled with dizziness, but this has all passed away. I can heartily recommend the Columbian to any one afflicted as I have been.   W. S. TURNER, Tallmadge Ave., North Hill.

Can cheerfully recommend it to be all you claim for it.   W. A. RODGERS, 4312 Butler St., Pittsburg, Pa.

Gained 10 pounds the first three weeks. I feel that it would be cheap at $10.   W. A. HEACOCK, Alliance, O.

I can not say enough in praise of Columbian Remedy.   D. J. WELTON, 408½ W. Center St., Akron, O.

I think it is the best medicine I ever took.   REV. S. S. PENWOOD, Bedford, Ind.

BETTER THAN DOCTORS.

Columbian Medicine Company: TWINSBURG, O., December 11th, 1892.

GENTLEMEN:—I have been taking your medicine and it has done more for me than all the doctors' medicine I ever took, trouble was pain in my side and head.   Yours truly,   G. A. LUKE.

ALL IT IS CLAIMED TO BE.

Columbian Medicine Company: S. AMHERST, O., LORAIN CO., Dec. 12th, 1892.

GENTLEMEN:—Have used one box of your remedy and can say it is all it is claimed to be. It has done me more good than anything I have taken this long time; find enclosed $1.00 for a box for my mother; send soon as possible.   MR. HARRETT BUNCE.

GREATLY BENEFITTED.

Columbian Medicine Company: AKRON, O., December 14th, 1892.

GENTLEMEN:—About three weeks ago I bought from your agent, J. W. Hudson, a box of Columbian remedy. I have been a great sufferer from obstinate constipation, but since taking your medicine I am greatly benefitted, and would highly recommend the Columbian Remedy to anyone similarly afflicted.   HARRY MUNSON, with Geo. Billow.

PIGEON PIE.—Take half a dozen pigeons, stuff each one with a dressing the same as for turkey; loosen the joints with a knife, but do not separate them. Put them in a stew pan with water enough to cover them, let them cook until nearly tender, then season them with salt and pepper and butter. Thicken the gravy with flour, remove and cool. Butter a pudding dish, line the sides with a rich crust. Have ready some hard boiled eggs cut in slices. Put in a layer of eggs and birds and gravy until the dish is full, cover with a crust and bake.

ROAST QUAIL—Rinse well and steam over boiling water until tender, then dredge with flour and smother in butter; season with salt and pepper and roast inside the stove; thicken the gravy, serve with green grape jelly and garnish with parsley.

MEATS.

All pieces of meat, unless very salt, should be plunged into boiling water and boiled rapidly for 15 minutes to harden the albumen that is on the outside, and thus keep in the juices. The kettle should then be put back where it will just simmer, for meat that is boiled rapidly becomes hard and stringy. A good way is to thickly flour a piece of coarse cloth, pin the meat in it, and place in the boiling water.

BOILED HAM.—The New York "Tribune" gives these directions for boiling ham: Soak the ham all night in water, which should cover it entirely. Then set it on the fire to boil. The rule for boiling a ham is fifteen minutes to each pound, so you can easily tell by weighing it the exact length of time it will be necessary to cook it. When it is half boiled, change the water, and to the last boiling add a cupful of molasses. When it is done, set it to cool, and when it is cold enough, skin it and put it in the oven to bake until the whole is nicely browned.

STEWED LAMB CHOPS.—Cut three pounds of chops from a loin of lamb; trim, and put on to stew in enough

water to come around but not over it. Remove the scum as it rises, and keep well covered. When very tender, season with salt and pepper, and thicken with a tablespoonful each of flour and butter rubbed together. Have ready on a platter a few slices of buttered evenly brown toast; lay the pieces of meat on the toast, and pour the gravy over all.

BOILED CORN BEEF.—Wash and put into boiling water; cook very slowly for 2½ hours three pounds of the beef. If it is to be served cold, let it stand for ½ an hour in the water in which it was boiled.

BOILED SALT TONGUE.—Soak over night, and cook from five to six hours. Throw into cold water and peel off the skin.

FRESH BOILED TONGUE.- Put into boiling water enough to cover, with two tablespoonfuls of salt; cook same as salt tongue.

HAMBURG STEAK.—Have your butcher grind for you a pound of lean loin steak, with which as he grinds, he must put two ounces of good suet, mixing thoroughly; make into flat round cakes about ¾ inch thick and 2½ inches in diameter, firmly packed together. Lay these in a skillet in which a little suet or lard is previously heated very hot, fry till brown then turn when both sides are brown, dust salt and pepper on both sides and serve while hot. The cook must give undivided attention till they are done. Skillet must be kept as hot as possible without burning the meat; put no cover over them while cooking; cook only as long as it takes to broil an ordinary steak. This is an inexpensive and good dish of wholesome meat if directions are carefully followed.
MRS. LUCY K. BENNETT, AKRON, O.

VEAL CHOPS.—In frying veal chops sift on both sides with sugar before placing in hot butter.
MRS. IRA M. MILLER.

MOCK OYSTERS.—Take the cold veal left from dinner and cut in pieces about an inch thick. Dip in egg, roll in crackers and drop in boiling hot lard and brown.
MISS BROOKS.

METHOD OF PREPARING EGGS.—Boil the eggs hard. When cold take off the shells, cut in halves, take out the yolks, and mix with salt, pepper, mustard, a little parsley chopped fine, melted butter and a little vinegar. Put this mixture back into the whites garnished with parsley.

MRS. B. F. WHEELER.

MEAT CROQUETTES.—One pound chopped raw beef, one egg, one onion (or none), pepper and salt, mix, form in two small cakes, dredge with flour and fry in butter.

MRS. N. D. TIBBALS.

BAKED EGGS.—Break six into a buttered dish, taking care that each is whole, do not mix or disturb the yolks, sprinkle with pepper and salt, and put a bit of butter on each egg. Put in oven and bake until the whites are set. This is superior to fried eggs and very nice served on toast, sprigs of parsley alternating with currant jelly.

FRIED MUTTON CHOPS.—Place in a frying pan a good tablespoonful of butter and lard mixed. Dip each chop in rolled cracker crumbs and beaten egg. Sprinkle salt and pepper on both sides and fry brown.

BAKED MUTTON CHOPS AND POTATOES.—Slice some good potatoes about an eighth of an inch thick; the quantity to be determined by the number of persons to be served. Arrange in layers in a deep earthen dish, sprinkle salt and pepper between each layer and sufficient cold water to keep them from burning. Place in a hot oven and when nicely browned, place a number of mutton chops on top, add a little more salt and pepper and water if required and place in a cooler part of the oven for about forty minutes. Brown chops on both sides. If the potatoes become too dry while cooking add a little hot water from time to time. Serve hot.

IRISH STEW.—Three pounds mutton chops, a dozen medium sized potatoes, three turnips, two good sized onions and a quart of cold water. Place in a stew pan in alternate layers of vegetables and chops, pour the water over them and cook until all are thoroughly done or about one hour and a half.

FRIED SALT PORK.—Cut the pork into thin slices, roll in flour and fry crisp. If the pork should need freshening pour over it some boiling water, let it stand a short time, drain off the water, roll in flour and cook as before. If gravy is desired, a tablespoonful or two of flour may be stirred into the frying pan after the meat has been removed, a half pint of sweet milk, a dash of pepper and if too fresh a little salt. Chipped celery leaves or parsley adds a fine flavor.

BACON AND EGGS.—If any cold bacon and eggs are on hand they may be chopped together, mixed with cold mashed or fine chopped potatoes, mould into small cakes dipped in beaten egg and cracker crumbs, fried brown on both sides and serve hot.

FRIED SAUSAGES.—Prick the casing with a fork in order to keep it from bursting, or else pour a little cold water into the frying pan, let it come to a boil, pour off and fry ten or twelve minutes in about a dessert spoonful of hot butter, turn frequently.

BAKED SAUSAGES. — Sausages may be deliciously cooked by placing them in a pan and baking them in a hot oven about fifteen minutes, browning nicely on both sides.

BEEF STEAK.—Heat a thick bottomed frying pan very hot and drop into it about one teaspoonful of butter, put in the steak and turn continually until thoroughly done; place in a warm platter and season with butter, pepper and salt.

BEEF STEAK AND ONIONS.—Fry the steak and have ready some onions which have been nicely cooked in beef drippings or butter and cover thickly over the steak and serve.

BEEF STEAK AND OYSTERS.—One quart of oysters, heated, stir into them one-fourth of a pound of butter mixed with two tablespoonfuls of sifted flour and when it thickens pour over the fried steak and serve hot.

OLD FASHIONED POT ROAST.—For a family of five or six persons, take about three pounds of fresh beef, wash and place in a pot with just barely enough water to cover it, cook slowly about thirty minutes, then season with salt and pepper and a little onion (if desired) and cook slowly until

tender. If much gravy is left in the pot after the meat has become tender pour it off and put in some butter. Dredge the meat with flour and brown.

VEAL LOAF.—Four pounds chopped veal, ½ pound salt pork chopped fine, four eggs, four tablespoonfuls of bread crumbs. ½ pint milk, 1½ teaspoonfuls salt, three teaspoonfuls sage, ½ teaspoonful black pepper. Mix thoroughly, put into a bread pan, spread the top with butter and bake three hours.   MRS. FRANK MEACHAM.

BEEF LOAF.—Three pounds of chopped round steak, small piece of suet, two eggs, one cup of sweet milk, small lump of butter and one pint of cracker crumbs. Salt and pepper to suit taste. Mix thoroughly and make them into loaf shape and bake slowly 2½ hours, basting frequently.
                    MRS. GEORGE SHROCK.

GAME.

COOKING GAME.—Take your birds and pick them without scalding. *Never skin* them. Then split open the back so it will lay flat in the skillet, then wash them with as little water as you can, then salt and pepper on both sides, roll in flour, put on your skillet with about twice as much lard as butter and when very hot put birds in. Brown on both sides a dark brown. When they are nice and brown pour hot water over them, enough to cover well. Put a tight lid on to keep all the steam in. You can let them cook slowly for about half to three-quarters of an hour. You can have toast to put on the plate to put the birds on with the gravy; add more water if necessary. This is the best way to cook quail or woodcock.   MRS. R. B. MORGAN.

VEGETABLES.

BAKED BEANS.—One quart of small white beans, soaked over night. In the morning change the water, pour on boiling water, add a pinch of soda, one pound of salt

THE HANKEY LUMBER CO., Lumber, C. A. Hankey, President; J. F.
Stuver, Secretary; F. H. Weeks, General Manager and Treasurer; No. 1036 South
Main Street. A successful and prominent concern in Akron, actively engaged in the
manufacture of lumber and interior woodwork, is that known as The Hankey Lumber
Co., whose office and planing mill are located at No. 1036 South Main Street. This
business was established in 1873 by S. Hankey, who conducted it until 1885 when his
death occurred, and was carried on by Mrs. C. A. Hankey until 1889, when it was duly
incorporated with a paid up capital of $100,000. the chief executive officers being Mrs.
C. A. Hankey, president; W. S. Hankey, Vice-President; Mr. J. F. Stuver, secretary;
and Mr. F. H. Weeks, general manager and treasurer. The grounds and planing mill
have an area of four acres. The planing mill is a spacious two-story building, fully
equipped with the latest improved wood working machinery, tools and appliances
known to the trade. Here a strong force of hands are employed, and the machinery is
driven by a superior eighty horse-power steam-engine. The Hankey Lumber Co.
deals largely in all kinds of lumber both at wholesale and retail, and also manufac-
tures sash, doors, blinds, frames, mouldings and all kinds of inside woodwork. They
enjoy intimate associations with manufacturers and shippers of lumber, and as all
supplies are received direct from the forests and mill, they are enabled to offer the
trade superior advantages in prices and quality of lumber. A stock of 2,000,000 feet of
choice lumber is constantly on hand, and the sales for the past year amounted to
5,000,000 feet. The company also promptly furnishes estimates and contracts for the
building of houses, stores, etc., in Akron and its vicinity. The officers are highly re-
garded in trade circles for their enterprise, business capacity and integrity, and the
prospects of the company, under their able guidance, are of the most favorable char-
acter.

fat pork, boil until nearly tender; add one tablespoonful of brown sugar, place in a crock and bake.

MRS. N. D. TIBBALS.

BAKED PORK AND BEANS.—Take three pints of white beans and soak over night. Pour off the water, add clear water and parboil till the skin will crack by blowing on them ; put them in a bean pot with two table spoonfuls of molasses, a little salt and pepper, and a pound of pork at the top. Fill with water, keep adding water for four hours, then let them bake slowly for four hours more.

MRS. W. H. ROOK.

CABBAGE.—A good-sized dish. Two eggs, two table-spoonfuls of sugar, butter the size of an egg, 1½ cups of vin-egar. Beat the butter and sugar, then add the vinegar and boil one minute, stirring often. Remove from fire and stir in whipped eggs very slowly. Sprinkle a teaspoonful of mustard on the cabbage, with pepper and salt. Pour the mixture on the cabbage boiling hot. MRS. G. C. BERRY.

CANNED CORN.— Take nice tender green corn, cut from the cob with a sharp knife ; with the back of the knife scrape the cob so as to get all the sweetness possible; see that your jars are perfect, no cracks; put in the corn and with the small end of a potato masher pack it in. A quart jar will take twelve or thirteen ordinary ears. When the jar is plump full, put on the rubbers and screw almost perfectly tight. Put hay or cloths in the bottom of the wash boiler, lay in the cans of corn in any way you please; put little cloths in to keep them from hitting each other, fill the boiler as full as you wish; cover over with cold water and set it over the fire. When it begins to boil, boil three hours with-out ceasing. Then take out and with your tightener make as tight as possible immediately. After they are cold tight-en again if you can. Put away in a cool, dark place.

MRS. LEWIS MILLER.

COLD SLAW.—Slice your cabbage as fine as you can, pound enough to start the juice and when it seems wilted; then beat and pour over hot, ½ cup of vinegar, the same of sugar, butter and milk, yolks of two eggs, and cover up to steam. In summer it need not be covered.

COLD SLAW.—Cook to a cream ½ cup of butter, ½ cup of vinegar. ½ cup of milk, ¼ cup of sugar, one tablespoonful of corn starch. two eggs and pour over one head of cabbage.

MRS. A. M. HEATHMAN.

PARSNIP FRITTERS.—Boil four or five parsnips; when tender take off the skin and mash them fine; add to them a teaspoonful of wheat flour and a beaten egg; put a table-spoonful of lard or beef dripping in a frying pan; add to it a salt-spoonful of salt. When boiling hot make in small cakes with a spoon. When one side is a delicate brown, turn; when both are done, take them on a dish, put a very little of the fat in which they were fried over them and serve hot.

MRS. E. LONG.

POTATO CROQUETTES.—Two cups of cold mashed pota-to, egg, lump of butter half the size of an egg, salt to taste, and ½ cup of rolled crackers. Shape with the hand into balls or cakes, roll in a little flour and fry in hot lard as dough-nuts. AGNES P. BURTON.

SAUER-KRAUT.—For six gallons of fine chopped cab-bage, use one cup of salt. Pound it in the crock until the froth comes on top. Put on a weight and set in a warm place. MRS. WM. ROOK.

CABBAGE SALAD.—Two quarts of finely chopped cab-bage, two level tablespoonfuls of salt, two of white sugar, one of black pepper and a heaping one of ground mustard; rub yolks of four hard boiled eggs until smooth, add ¼ cup butter, slightly warmed; mix thoroughly with the cabbage, and add a teacup of vinegar. Serve with the whites of the eggs sliced and placed on the salad.

CREAM SLAW.—One gallon cabbage cut very fine, pint vinegar, pint sour cream, half cup of sugar, teaspoonful of flour, two eggs and a piece of butter the size of a walnut; put vinegar, sugar and butter in the same pan and let boil; stir eggs, cream and flour previously well mixed. into the vinegar, boil thoroughly, and put over the cabbage, sprinkle with one tablespoonful of salt, one of black pepper and one of mustard.

PLAIN COLD SLAW.—Slice cabbage very fine, season with salt; pepper and a little sugar, pour over vinegar and

mix thoroughly. It is nice served in the center of a platter with fried oysters around it. CYNTHIA ROTHROCK,
Des Moines, Iowa.

BROWNED POTATOES.— Take small potatoes, parboil, and fry in butter.

POTATO STRIPS.—Peal, cut in long strips, and lay in cold water one hour and dry and fry in salted lard. Place in collander to dry. Lay a napkin under them when served. Do not crowd in frying.

POTATO CROQUETTES.—Season cold mashed potatoes with pepper and salt; beat to a cream; add a teaspoonful of melted butter and one egg to every cup of potato.

POTATO CROQUETTES.—Take two cups of cold mashed potatoes, season with a pinch of salt and pepper and a table-spoonful of butter; beat up the whites of two eggs and work all together thoroughly. Make into small balls, dip them into the beaten yolks of the eggs and roll into either flour or cracker crumbs and fry in hot butter or lard.

TO BOIL NEW POTATOES.—Do not have the potatoes dug until you are ready to use them. Wash them well and remove the skins and put in boiling salted water. Cook until tender. When done pour off the water. Raise the cover of the sauce-pan just a little to allow the steam to escape and the potatoes to dry thoroughly. Place them in a hot vegetable dish with small pieces of butter. Serve hot.

MASHED POTATOES.—Take the quantity of potatoes needed, pare, and allow to stand in cold salt water 30 minutes, boil until tender and mash fine with a potato-masher. Have ready a piece of butter the size of an egg melted in half a cup of hot milk or more if needed (butter and milk.)

FRIED POTATOES.—Peel a quantity of potatoes, slice them very thin, put a tablespoonful each of butter and lard into a frying pan, put in the potatoes and season with pepper and salt, cover with a tight-fitting lid and let the steam almost cook them, then take off the cover and let them fry a light brown.

ESCALLOPED POTATOES.—Peel and slice thin the quantity of potatoes needed. Butter an earthen dish, put in a layer of potatoes and season with salt, pepper and butter

Mount + Union + College,

ALLIANCE, OHIO.

DEPARTMENTS:—Preparatory, Collegiate, Post-Graduate, Normal, Business, Music, Fine Art, Biblical, Military.

EVERY DEPARTMENT fully equipped and never in better condition. Attendance last year 594, the largest for years.

ADVANTAGES :—Four Term Plan, Noted Museum, Library and Reading Room, Gymnasium and Observatory, Elective Courses, Literary Societies.

The whole expense at Mt. Union College is very low, compared with that of other colleges; it is really as low as any and lower than many. An education can be secured here for about one-half what it costs at some colleges. Some young people can live here more cheaply than at home. In calculating the expenses of a college, the special advantages by way of extra privileges, opportunities, appliances, conveniences, should be considered. No college offers equal extra benefits together with efficient instruction for less expense. . . . .

TERM OPEN.—Summer, May 2, 1893.

For further information send for catalogue, or write to President Marsh.

and a bit of chopped onion (if liked). Now put another layer of potatoes and thus continue until the dish is filled. Before putting into the oven pour enough hot milk over them to nearly cover. Bake about ¾ of an hour. Cold boiled potatoes may be done the same and chopped parsley or celery may be substituted for the onion if preferred.

SWEET POTATOES, A LA PROVINCE.—Slice raw sweet potatoes thin and lay in a dish with bits of butter. Sprinkle with salt and pepper, pour over milk to cover; wet bread crumbs in cream, add a beaten egg and pour over the top and bake until done.

SWEET POTATOES.—For a mess of sweet potatoes wash clean and boil with the skins on in salt water. When done, peel and slice in two length-wise. Fill a baking dish and sprinkle with sugar, butter, pepper and salt. Bake until brown.   MRS. HERMAN PRANGE.

BOILED ONIONS.—Peel the onions and place in cold water in a stew-pan and let them scald for a few minutes, then turn off that water and cover with fresh cold water salted a little. Boil slowly until tender, then dry. Pour little melted butter over them. Sprinkle with pepper and salt and serve hot.

ESCALLOPED ONIONS.—Boil onions tender, lay them in a baking dish with alternate layers of bread crumbs seasoned with bits of butter, pepper and salt, putting a layer of bread crumbs last. Pour over them some hot milk and bake 20 minutes.

CORN FRITTERS.—Take a can of corn, add a little butter, pepper and salt and thicken with flour mixed with one teaspoonful of baking powder. Have some lard boiling and drop in.   MISS MARY BROOKS.

BOILED GREEN CORN.—In cooking green corn which has been picked some time previous, a little sugar should be put into the water in which it is being boiled (about one tablespoonful is enough). Take off the husks and silk and boil about thirty minutes in unsalted water. The flavor is improved by boiling with husks on.

FRIED EGG PLANT. — Slice the egg plant quite thin and soak in cold water 20 minutes, then dip in cracker

crumbs and beaten egg and fry in hot butter until a light brown.

STEWED CELERY.—Boil same as green corn, then add butter, salt, pepper and milk or cream.

BOILED SQUASH.—Wash them and cut them into pieces, take out the seeds, boil until tender, when done drain and squeeze them until all the water has been pressed out, mash them with little butter, pepper and salt; then put the squash into a stew pan, place over the fire and stir frequently until it becomes dry, taking care not to let it burn.

BAKED SQUASH.—Cut open the squash and take out the seeds and without paring cut into large pieces, place in a dripping pan in a moderately hot oven and bake about an hour, when done it may be peeled and mashed like potatoes or serve the pieces on a hot dish to be eaten with butter like sweet potatoes.

ASPARAGUS WITH CREAM.—Have the asparagus tied in bundles, wash and place into boiling water in which there is a teaspoonful of salt for every quart of water, boil rapidly for 15 minutes, take it up and cut off tender heads, put them in a sauce pan with a generous cup of cream or milk for every quart of asparagus, simmer ten minutes, mix one tablespoonful of butter and a teaspoonful of flour and stir into the asparagus, add salt and pepper to taste and simmer five minutes longer.

STEWED CARROTS.—Clean the parsnips and divide into strips, put them into a stew pan with water enough to cover them, add a little salt and boil until tender, then drain and replace them in the pan with two tablespoonfuls of butter rolled in flour, shake over a little pepper and salt, add enough cream or milk to moisten the whole and let it come to a boil and serve hot.

SPINACH.—It must be carefully picked and washed in several waters, drain in a collander, put into a large sauce pan with only the water that adheres to it, let it simmer slowly for about an hour, drain and dish it; spread over the spinach a lump of butter, and season with pepper and salt; slice a couple of hard boiled eggs, and place the pieces over the top.   Serve hot.

SALADS AND SAUCES.

CHICKEN SALAD.--Two large chickens boiled tender; six good sized heads of celery; chop and mix together. One pound of butter and two tablespoons mustard mixed together. Stir to a smooth paste, add one heaping spoon of salt, three ounces of sugar, and the yolks of ten eggs, beaten lightly. Stir this all to a cream; then warm about a pint of vinegar, and stir a little into the other ingredients, just enough to soften it. When the balance of the vinegar is hot, stir the mixture into it, stirring constantly until it thickens. When cold, pour over the chicken. This makes two gallons or a little more.   MRS. NETTIE MCNAUGHTON.

CHICKEN SALAD WITHOUT CELERY.—One pint chopped chickens, one pint cabbage chopped very fine, two eggs beaten light, ½ pint cream or rich milk, two tablespoonfuls of sugar, one of mustard, four of vinegar, one teaspoonful of celery seed, a little salt and pepper, and butter the size of a walnut. Stir the eggs, sugar, mustard, &c., together, and place over the fire, stirring constantly until it boils. When cold pour over the chicken and cabbage.
                        L. M. STORER.

POTATO SALAD.—Boil a dozen potatoes. When cold pare and slice thin; also slice fine half an onion. Cut up a little piece of smoked bacon and let fry a few moments, take out the little bits, pour in a pint of vinegar, and let it get hot. Butter is used oftentimes instead of bacon; a piece of butter the size of a hickory nut. When melted add vinegar, and when nearly cooled, pour over the potatoes. Have salt and pepper on the potatoes; put in a little parsley; mix just before serving.   MRS. LEWIS MILLER.

SALAD DRESSING.—One tablespoonful of flour, one tablespoonful of mustard, two tablespoonfuls of cream, six teaspoonfuls of vinegar, two eggs well beaten, butter size of an egg, salt and pepper. Beat well together, and cook till quite thick. Cut the lobster into small pieces, and mix with it salt and pepper. Pour over the dressing just before sending to the table. Garnish with celery tops, whites of eggs and the small clams.   MRS. KING.

CHILI SAUCE.—Twelve large tomatoes peeled, three green peppers. Chop fine separately, then add one teacupful of sugar, two of vinegar, two tablespoonfuls of salt, teaspoonful of allspice, and one tablespoonful of ground cinnamon. Boil down till of the consistency of catsup.

MRS. A. JACKSON.

CHILI SAUCE.—Eighteen large tomatoes, half ripe, four onions and ten peppers all chopped fine, four cups vinegar, four tablespoonfuls sugar, two tablespoonfuls each of salt, cloves, cinnamon and allspice. Boil one hour. Bottle while hot.

MRS. J. F. HOY.

GOVERNOR SAUCE.—Chop a peck of green tomatoes, six green peppers and four onions, (you have to chop the peppers separately). Mix together with one cup of salt, let stand over night, put them in the colander to drain well, then add one quart of horse radish, one cup of sugar, vinegar enough to boil it in, and boil.

MRS. G. D. BATES.

MUSTARD SAUCE.—Yolks of five eggs, four teaspoons mustard, ½ cup of butter, one glass sour jelly, (many prefer it without jelly), four tablespoons sugar, salt, pepper and vinegar to taste. Cook till the eggs are done.

OLLIE WALLACE.

OYSTER SAUCE.—Put the oysters into a sauce pan, pour in the strained liquor and let them heat slowly, but not boil. After they have simmered a few minutes take out the oysters, mix a quarter of a pound of fresh butter with a tablespoonful of flour. Stir these into the liquor until it boils, and there is no fear of lumps; then pour in by degrees a breakfastcupful of cream. Keep the sauce stirred until it shows symptoms of boiling, then add the oysters and cayenne pepper. The sauce must simmer until wanted. Serve with roast fowl.

MRS. G. D. BATES.

COLD SLAW.—One half pint vinegar, tablespoonful butter, two tablespoonfuls flour, two eggs, one teacup sweet milk, a little red pepper and mustard. Salt the cabbage in the dish and pour over the liquid boiling hot.

F. E. BABBITT.

SLAW DRESSING.—One teaspoonful of mustard and egg and three tablespoonfuls of water, three of sugar, ¾ cup of sweet milk. ¾ of vinegar, set on the stove until it thickens; stirring all the time but not let it boil, then have cabbage ready and sprinkle a tablespoonful of celery and mustard seed over it and pepper and salt to suit the taste; pour dressing over it while hot. MRS. WM. PHILLIPS.

STEAMED CABBAGE.—Take a sound, solid cabbage and cut very finely: put it in a sauce-pan; pour in a half tea cup full of water or enough to keep from burning, cover tightly, add a little water now and then until it begins to be tender, then put into it a large tablespoonful of butter, salt and pepper to taste, and if desired a third of a cup of vinegar may be added.

BOILED PARSNIPS.—Wash and scrape, and cut them. Place in boiling water, add a little salt and boil them until quite tender. Dry them and pour melted butter over them or (sauce). Mix one tablespoonful of sifted flour with ¼ of a cup of melted butter; heat to boiling ½ pint sweet milk, stir into it the butter and flour and season with pepper and salt.

STUFFED BAKED TOMATOES.—Take ½ dozen, or more as may be needed, of good-sized tomatoes; cut a slice from the blossom end and carefully remove the pulp, then fill the shell with the following: Chop some cabbage and onion very finely together, mix with bread or cracker crumbs and the tomato pulp which has been removed, season with pepper, salt, sugar and sweet milk or cream; then replace the slices, place in buttered pan with just water enough to keep from burning, and bake until done.

CUCUMBER A LA CREME.—Peel and cut into long strips some fine cucumbers, boil in salt water until soft and serve with cream sauce.

ESCALLOPED TOMATOES.—Put in a pan a layer of tomatoes, put on pepper, salt and butter. Sprinkle with bread crumbs. So on till the pan is full, the last layer to be bread crumbs. MISS BROOKS.

CELERY SAUCE.—Clean and cut into small pieces. cook until tender. Dress with cream, butter, and a little thickening. MRS. HERMAN PRANGE.

BOILED SALAD DRESSING.—Four eggs, whites and yolks beaten separately. two teaspoonfuls of mustard, two teaspoonfuls of salt. three teaspoonfuls sugar, one cup vinegar, boil until thick, two tablespoonfuls butter, a little chopped onion lastly. MATTIE B.

MAYONAISE DRESSING.—One tablespoonful of mustard, one teaspoonful of sugar, ¼ teaspoonful of cayenne pepper, one teaspoonful salt, yolk of three eggs, ¼ cup vinegar, ½ pint of oil. one cup whipped cream. Beat the yolk and other ingredients until they are very light and thick. Add a few drops of oil at a time until the dressing becomes thick and rather hard. After it has reached this stage the oil can be added more rapidly. When it gets very thick add a little vinegar. When the last of the oil and vinegar has been added it should be very thick. Now add the whipped cream, or it can be omitted without injury.

SALMON SALAD.—Open the can, drain off the oil, fill the can with vinegar and set in a pan of boiling water, to remain an hour; drain off all the liquor and set in a cool place. Dressing: To one can of salmon beat two eggs till very light; pour over them half a teacupful of boiling vinegar and set on the fire until it thickens; add a teaspoonful of butter, some mustard and cayenne pepper; set away to cool. When ready for the table add five teaspoonfuls of sweet cream and dress with lettuce. MATTIE BREWSTER.

CUCUMBER SALAD.—Take a platter and garnish with crisp leaves of lettuce. Put a layer of sliced tomatoes, then a layer of sliced cucumbers.
Dressing: One-half cup mashed potatoes. two hardboiled eggs rubbed to a paste. one tablespoonful butter, pepper, salt, mustard and a grated onion. Boil one beaten egg in ½ teacupful of vinegar and pour over the potatoes and onion, and pour all over the tomatoes and cucumbers. MISS BROOKS.

BREADS.

Knead late in the evening. A teacup and a half of yeast will make eight loaves. To this quantity of yeast take one gallon of warm milk, one half teacup of sugar, butter or lard

size of an egg, a handful of salt, and flour enough to make stiff. Let rise until morning. Bake ¾ of an hour.

MRS. LEWIS MILLER.

BREAD WITHOUT MILK.—Boil two medium-sized pota-toes in a quart of water. When done take out and mash fine, add a teaspoonful each of salt and sugar, pour on the boiling potato water and *immediately* stir in flour enough to make a thick batter. Let it cool, then put in it any good yeast. One cake of dry yeast is about the right quantity. When fully light, knead your bread, using all the sponge, or you can save a little, (in cool weather) for yeast next time if you wish. Let rise, mold into loaves, let rise again and bake. This makes two large loaves. Should you wish to make more or less, vary the quantity of sponge accordingly. Al-ways have enough of it, so as to have no other wetting.

MRS. E. W. GAYLORD.

BROWN BREAD.—Heat together two teaspoonfuls of mo-lasses, one of soda, and one of salt, when light take from the fire and add one quart of sweet milk, or half milk and half water, and two teaspoonfuls of baking powder mixed with flour; add enough more graham to make batter as if for corn cakes.

MRS. DR. FISHER.

BROWN BREAD.—Two cups of rye meal, two cups of corn meal, one cup of molasses. Scald half a cup of the corn meal, add two cups of sour milk and one teaspoonful of saleratus. Boil three hours in a tin pail in water.

MRS. WM. ROOK.

COFFEE BREAD.—One-half cup of sugar, two eggs, two cups of milk, four cups of flour, three teaspoonfuls baking powder and a little salt. Bake in a quick oven in a flat tin.

MRS. B. F. WHEELER.

CORN BREAD.—Three cups of sifted meal, 1½ cups of boiled rice, four eggs well beaten, 3½ cups of sour milk, one tablespoonful melted butter, one teaspoonful soda dissolved in hot water, salt. Bake in two or three pans.

CORN BREAD.—One quart of corn meal made into mush. When cold add one pint of sugar, 1½ cups of good yeast. Mix thoroughly and thicken with flour and raise in a warm

place over night. Then add flour to mold into loaves, place in pans, and after raising again, bake in a hot oven.

MRS. C. S. FARRAR.

GOOD YEAST RAISING.—Boil a handful of hops in two quarts of water ten minutes, then strain and add six good sized potatoes, grated, one cup of sugar, one tablespoonful of salt. Let the potatoes and hop water simmer ½ hour, when lukewarm add one cup of good yeast, let it rise. This is the best recipe I have ever tried for making jug yeast. It should be kept in a cool place. MARY PIKE.

RELIABE MODUS OPERANDI.—First place in a cup of tepid water, 1½ yeast cakes ("Yeast Foam" has always proved good.) Pare carefully three or four medium-sized potatoes and boil in a quart of water. When thoroughly done remove the water and mash and press through a soup strainer or fine sieve; then pour the potato water over it; when it has cooled stir in the yeast which has dissolved in the warm water. Stir into this enough flour to make a firm batter, let rise over night. In the morning put into the bread tray five quarts of flour and mix into it about three quarts of tepid water, stir thoroughly as possible with a spoon, then knead well with the hands for about twenty minutes. Set in a warm place to rise, which will require from two to three hours. Then mould into loaves and let it stand until light; then bake in a moderate oven for an hour. This recipe is sufficient for six loaves of bread.

GRAHAM BREAD.—One quart of graham flour, a pinch of salt, two level tablespoonfuls of granulated sugar, two teaspoonfuls cream of tartar and one teaspoonful of soda. Stir these thoroughly into the flour and mix with sweet milk to a *stiff* batter. Bake in a moderate oven. Cold water may be used instead of milk. MRS. W. A. PARDEE.

LIGHT BREAD.—Boil three large potatoes, drain the water off, mash them fine, then pour the water over them again and leave them set until cool. Put on water so when done there will be a pint, then take three heaping teaspoonfuls of flour, three of sugar and the same of salt, two pints

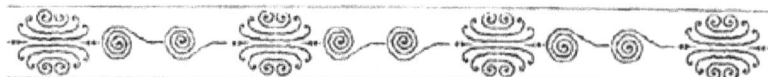

of cold water, mix smooth then leave until the potatoes are cold. Then put together and put in your yeast with it.

MRS. LOIS YERRICK.

GRAHAM BREAD.— To a small bowl of bread sponge, put one quart milk and water ½ of each; one large spoonful molasses.one of sugar, one teaspoonful soda, one teaspoonful salt, mix this together and stiffen with graham flour a little stiffer than cake, let rise like other loaves and bake.

MRS. F. MEACHAM.

DELICATE CORN BREAD.—One pint of sour or sweet milk, one teaspoonful of soda or baking powder, one table-spoonful of lard, a pinch of salt, stir in meal enough to make a batter the consistency of sponge cake.

MRS. IDA REX.

CORN BREAD.—Three cups white sponge, one cup Indian meal scalded, one half cup brown sugar, knead, then place in pans to raise. MRS. N. D. TIBBALS.

CORN BREAD.—Two eggs, one cup of sugar, ½ cup of melted butter, two cups of flour, one cup corn meal sifted, one cup of sweet milk, three teaspoonfuls baking powder, beat the eggs separately and add the whites the last thing.

MARY PIKE.

RYE BREAD.—Rye bread is easily made. That which is generally sold is made in the same way as an ordinary household loaf, but composed of equal quantities of rye flour and wheaten flour. It is said to improve the mixing if about one-eighth of its bulk of Indian corn is added. When this addition is made, every pound of Indian corn flour should be scalded first, by having a pint of boiling water thrown upon it and stirring it well, and when it has cooled down to a new milk warm temperature, it should be added to the rye and wheaten flours, and the mixing process pro-ceeded with as usual.

BISCUITS, GEMS, ROLLS, ETC.

GRAHAM BISCUIT.—Take three cups graham flour, one cup wheat flour, two large teaspoonfuls baking powder, well mixed with the flour, rub in two large tablespoonfuls of butter. a little salt. ½ cup sugar, one beaten egg and enough cold milk to make a soft dough, roll out, cut with biscuit cutter and bake in a quick oven.   MRS. MEACHAM.

GEMS.—One pint warm water, one teaspoonful of salt, graham flour enough to make a stiff batter. Have your irons and oven both hot.

GRAHAM PUFFS. One quart of graham flour, one pint of milk, one pint of water, two eggs and a little salt, bake in cups or gem pan.

POP OVERS.—One cup of flour, one cup of milk, one egg. piece of butter size of an egg, a little salt, one teaspoonful baking powder, to be baked in hot iron gem pans in a very quick oven. This rule makes twelve.
                            MRS. FRANK MASON.

TEA ROLLS.—Boil one pint of new sweet milk, add one-half cup of shortening, (¼ butter ¼ lard), and ¼ of a cup of sugar, when cool add ½ cup of soft yeast, a pinch of salt and enough flour to make a stiff batter, let rise until morning, mix, let it rise again, before meal time, roll out and cut with a biscuit cutter, make them long or round, let rise again, and then bake about twenty minutes; avoid too much flour. If directions are closely followed the result will be perfect.
                    MISS NELLIE ELLIS, Greenville, Pa.

MUFFINS.—One cup of sweet milk, ½ cup melted butter, one egg, two tablespoonfuls sugar, three teaspoonfuls of baking powder, flour to make a little thicker than cake batter.   ELLEN S. FUNK.

BUCKWHEAT CAKES.—One pint of warm water, three of buckwheat flour, one of flour, a little salt, one teacup of yeast. Let rise over night, in the morning before baking dissolve ½ teaspoonful soda in one teacup of warm water.
                            MRS. A. JACKSON.

BUCKWHEAT CAKES are improved a hundred per cent. by putting mashed potato in when you stir them for breakfast. Put a teaspoonful or two of soda in a little warm water, and stir in gently just before baking.

MRS. ELIZA WEARY.

CORN CAKES. --One pint corn meal. two tablespoonfuls wheat flour, one cup of white sugar, one teaspoonful salt, three teaspoonfuls baking powder, one egg, butter the size of an egg. Mix rapidly and thoroughly with one pint of sweet milk; bake twenty minutes. MRS. B. F. WHEELER.

FRENCH TOAST.--Put six slices of bread in a dish, beat two eggs well, and put in one pint of sweet milk. Stir well, pour over the bread, and let stand 10 minutes. Then bake on a hot buttered griddle, same as pancakes, and eat with butter and sugar, or syrup. MRS. N. A. MEANS.

GRAHAM GEMS.--One cup sweet milk, one egg, three teaspoonfuls baking powder, two tablespoonfuls sugar, two tablespoonfuls melted butter, a little salt, and $2\frac{1}{2}$ cups graham flour. Bake in gem pans. MRS. BECK.

GRAHAM PUFFS.--One egg, one pint sweet milk, one pint graham flour, a pinch of salt. Beat the whole briskly and bake quickly in gem pans. MRS. J. P. MARTIN.

HAM SANDWICHES.--Cut some slices of bread in a neat shape, and trim off the crust. Butter them and lay between some thin slices of cold ham, or ground, if you prefer, spread with mustard, if you like, and press hard.

MUFFINS.--Three eggs, three cups milk, four cups of flour and a little salt. Bake in muffin tins.

MRS. S. C. DYKE.

MUFFINS.--One quart milk, four eggs, $\frac{1}{2}$ cup of sugar, $\frac{1}{2}$ cup of butter, flour enough to make a batter of medium thickness. One teaspoonful of baking powder to each coffee cup of flour, salt to taste. MRS. DOWNEY.

BREAKFAST CAKES.--Two cups milk, two eggs, four cups flour, a little salt, four tablespoonfuls of melted butter, two of sugar, three teaspoonfuls baking powder.

ANNIE C. PRICE.

No other Life Policies as liberal cost as little money.

No other as cheap or give as much for the money as those of

- THE =

TRAVELERS!

Of Hartford, Conn.

NON-FORFEITABLE AND WORLD-WIDE.

ASSETS, - - $15,029,921.09
SURPLUS, - - 2,579,794.24

Also Chief Accident Company of the World.

Only large one in America.   Covers Accidents
of travel, sport or business all over the Globe.

PAYS POLICY-HOLDERS OVER $1,700,000 A YEAR.

H. P. HITCHCOCK, Agent,

TELEPHONE 194.   **200 E. Market St., Akron, O.**

Also represents the leading American and European
Fire Companies.

RELISH FOR BREAKFAST OR LUNCH.—Take a fourth of a pound of cheese, good and fresh; cut it up in thin slices, and put it in a spider, turning over it a large cup full of sweet milk; add a fourth of a teaspoonful of dry mustard, a little pepper and salt, and a piece of butter the size of an egg. Stir the mixture all the time. Have at hand three Boston crackers, finely powdered or rolled, and sprinkle them in gradually; as soon as they are stirred in turn out the contents into a warm dish and serve. It is very delicious.   MRS. J. F. HOY.

SALLIE LUNN.—One pint of flour, one egg, butter the size of an egg, one cup of milk, two heaping tablespoonfuls of light brown sugar, two tablespoonfuls of baking powder, a pinch of salt. Sift the baking powder into the flour, bake in a quick oven.

SAUCE FOR SALLIE LUNN.—Three heaping tablespoonfuls of sugar, $1\frac{1}{2}$ tablespoonfuls of butter, one tablespoonful of flour, a little nutmeg. Stir together and pour one pint of boiling water over it; cook five minutes.
                         MRS. SIMPSON.

STRAWBERRY SHORTCAKE.—One egg, one teaspoonful of butter, two tablespoonfuls of baking powder, $\frac{1}{4}$ cup of sweet milk, flour to make a soft dough. Make in cakes, bake on top of each other, when done take apart and place the strawberries between.

CORN MUFFINS.—One cup of corn meal, one cup flour, one cup sour milk, one teaspoonful of soda dissolved in milk, $\frac{1}{4}$ cup of butter, $\frac{1}{2}$ cup of sugar, two eggs, cream, butter and sugar; add well-beaten eggs, then milk and flour and meal sifted together. Bake in a quick oven.
                         MRS. H. J. SHREFFLER.

MUFFINS.—One cup of yellow corn meal, $\frac{1}{2}$ cup of flour, one tablespoonful of sugar, $1\frac{1}{2}$ teaspoonfuls of baking powder, one beaten egg, $1\frac{1}{2}$ cups sweet milk and a little salt. Bake in hot greased gem pans.   IDA M. MOORE.

RICE PANCAKES.—Boil one cup of rice. When boiled add three eggs, $\frac{1}{2}$ cup of flour. Mix well with sweet milk until thin enough to bake, add a little salt and sugar.
                         MISS ESTELLA SCHUBERT.

WAFFLES.—One pint of flour, one teaspoonful of baking powder, ½ teaspoonful of salt, four eggs, 1½ cupfuls of milk, one tablespoonful of butter melted. Mix in the order given, add the beaten yolks with the milk, then the melted butter, and the whites last. Bake on hot, well-greased waffle-irons.

GRAHAM GEMS.—One and a half cup of sour milk, ½ cup sugar, one egg, butter the size of an egg, small teaspoonful soda, flour enough to make a batter. Bake slow.

JENNIE PHILLIPS.

JOHNNY CAKE.—Two eggs, three cups butter-milk or sour milk, ½ cup of lard, ½ cup brown sugar, one cup of flour, one teaspoonful soda, ½ teaspoonful of salt, three cups indian meal. MRS. F. MEACHAM.

SAND TARTS.—½ pound of butter, one pound sugar, one pound flour, one pound baking bowder, four eggs. Roll out thin and bake in hot oven. MRS. J. H. DELLENBERGER.

OATMEAL CAKES.—(Scotch.) Boil together two cupfuls water, one cup shortening (half butter and half lard.) Pour this over five cupfuls of the finest oatmeal in which has been stirred one teaspoonful salt. Mix with hands, roll very thin and bake in quick oven. JENNIE WADDELL.

PIES.

APPLE CUSTARD PIE.—Make a nice rich crust, pare and quarter nice tart apples, lay them in the pan even, take one well-beaten egg and ½ pint sweet milk, pour over the apple and sweeten to taste. Flavor with nutmeg and bake without upper crust. MRS. N. R. STEINER.

CREAM PIE.—Three eggs, saving whites of two for frosting, ½ cup of sugar, add two heaping tablespoonfuls of cornstarch, dissolved in milk, little salt, pour into two cups boiling milk with butter the size of a walnut melted in it, cook until stiff enough, flavor and turn into a baked crust. Beat the whites of two eggs to a stiff froth, add ½ cup of sugar, flavor, spread on top, put in oven and let slightly brown. MRS. OAKLEY C. HERRICK.

AKRON, OHIO.

CREAM PIE.—Boil ½ pint of milk. Beat together ½ cup of sugar, the yolk of one egg, ¼ cup of flour, three table-spoonfuls of cold milk, and a pinch of salt. Stir into the hot milk, let cook until it thickens, stirring constantly, flavor with lemon, and pour upon the crust which should be baked before the cream is made. Frost with the white of an egg same as lemon pie.   MRS. W. A. PARDEE.

LEMON PIE.—To grated rind and juice of two lemons add 1½ cups of sugar, two tablespoonfuls of flour and butter size of an egg, four eggs beaten separately, one pint of very rich milk. Stir all together. This makes two pies.
                              MRS. A. P. BALDWIN.

LEMON PIE.—Superior. Take a deep dish, grate into it the outside rind of two lemons, add to that 1½ cups of white sugar, two heaping teaspoonfuls of unsifted flour, or one of cornstarch; stir it well together, then add the yolks of three well-beaten eggs, beat this thoroughly, then add the juice of the lemons, two cups of water, and a piece of butter the size of a walnut. Set this on the fire in another dish containing boiling water and cook it until it thickens, like cold honey. Remove it from the fire and when cooled pour it into a deep pie-tin, lined with pastry; bake, and when done have ready the whites beaten stiff, with three table-spoonfuls of sugar. Spread this on top and return to the oven to set and brown slightly. This makes a deep, large-sized pie, and extra good.   MRS. GEORGE SCHROCK.

LEMON PIE.—Six eggs very well beaten, not separating yolks from whites; add one tablespoonful of water (cold), 1½ cups of sugar, (brown light) beating constantly, lastly add juice one lemon. Bake in one crust, brisk oven, not too hot, ought to bake in about ten minutes. As soon as the crust is well baked, if the center trembles when the pie is taken from the oven, the pie is more perfect.
                              MRS. N. B. STONE.

RAISIN PIE.—One full coffee cup of raisins, one full coffee cup of sugar, butter the size of a small egg; two or more spoonfuls of flour. Process: Seed the raisins, cover with water, stew 20 minutes or more until tender, add sugar and butter when half stewed; when nearly done thicken with

paste carefully stirred of flour and water. Bake as a tart in nice platter or granite tin. MRS. N. B. STONE.

LEMON PIE.—One lemon (grated rind and juice), three eggs (yolks), three cups of sugar, three cups water, three tablespoonfuls flour. Boil and pour into the crust of three pies and use the whites for frosting.

LEMON PIE.—Upper crust. Juice and grated rind of one lemon, one cup water, one tablespoonful corn starch, one cup sugar, one egg, piece of butter the size of a small egg. Boil the water, wet the cornstarch with cold water and stir in. When boiling pour on the sugar and butter. When cool add the egg and lemon and bake with under and upper crust. MRS. HOUSEL.

MINCE PIE.—Three pints chopped meat, six of apples, one pint of chopped suet, one teaspoonful pepper, four teaspoonfuls salt, one tablespoonful cloves, four tablespoonfuls cinnamon, two nutmegs, two pounds raisins, two pounds of currants, $\frac{1}{2}$ pound citron, $\frac{1}{2}$ pint butter, one pound brown sugar, one pint molasses, one quart boiled cider.
MRS. N. B. STONE.

CUSTARD PIE.—For a common sized pie. Beat two eggs and one tablespoonful flour together, add $\frac{1}{2}$ cup sugar, maple is best; a little salt and nutmeg, stir into one pint of lukewarm water or milk. Bake with a strong heat at first and finish more slowly. MARY J. MOHLER.

TART PIE.—Put a glass of jelly into a baked crust. Beat the whites of two eggs to a stiff froth, add $\frac{1}{2}$ cup of sugar, flavor and spread on top, put in oven and let slightly brown.
MRS. B. C. HERRICK.

GOOD AND CHEAP PIE CRUST.—One quart sifted flour; one teaspoonful of salt, two heaping teaspoonfuls of Baking Powder; mix thoroughly while dry and sift. Then add cold sweet milk enough to make a stiff dough, and roll out as usual. Use the "Pie Crust Glaze" on both the bottom and top crusts; as per following recipe. Some prefer less of the baking powder in pie crust; a trial will determine what quantity best suits your taste.

PIE CRUST GLAZE.—To prevent the juice soaking through into the crust and making it soggy, wet the crust with a beaten egg just before you put in the pie mixture. If the top of the pie is wet with the egg it gives it a beautiful brown.

BOSTON CREAM PIE.—Delicious for those who like custard. For the crust, three eggs, one cup sugar, one cup flour, one teaspoonful soda, two teaspoonfuls cream tartar. Bake in a quick oven. When done open it with a sharp knife, by cutting it horizontally between the top and bottom crusts, and spread with this custard: One pint of milk, three eggs, five tablespoonfuls of sugar, one teaspoonful flavoring.

MRS. G. C. BERRY.

COCOANUT PIE.—One cocoanut grated, yolks of four eggs, whites of two, $1\frac{1}{2}$ cups of butter, two cups sugar, $\frac{1}{2}$ cup flour, one quart sweet milk, one nutmeg grated. Save the whites for frosting. Beat all together, melt the butter, then add the milk. Bake like custard. This makes two pies.

MRS. H. HART.

CORNSTARCH PIE.—Tablespoonful cornstarch, two of sugar, two spoonfuls of milk, yolks of two eggs. Beat well together in a crock, warmed; stir in a pint of boiling milk; let it boil up. Then add a teaspoonful of lemon or vanilla and a pinch of salt. Have a crust baked; turn in mold hot; frost with the whites of eggs and a teaspoonful of sugar; return to oven and brown quickly.

MRS. Z. C. JONES.

CRANBERRY PIE.—Quart cranberries stewed well in a cup of water; stir in three cups of white sugar, while hot. Sprinkle a very little flour in each pie. Bake with two crusts. This makes three pies.

MRS. Z. C. JONES.

LEMON PIE.—Grate the rind and squeeze the juice of one lemon, add yolks of three eggs, $\frac{1}{2}$ teacup of sugar, teacup of water, two tablespoonfuls cornstarch. Make frosting of whites and spread on top. Bake a light brown. This makes two pies.

OLLIE WALLACE.

LEMON PIE.—Yolks of three eggs, white of one, a cup of sugar, a cup of boiling water, a tablespoonful of cornstarch, $1\frac{1}{2}$ lemons, (juice and grated rind), a small piece of

butter. For frosting: Whites of two eggs, five tablespoonfuls of pulverized sugar, juice of ½ lemon. Frost the pie
when cold and brown slightly. MRS. DOWNEY.

PUMPKIN PIE.—Cut your pumpkin in pieces, put in the
oven and bake, when done scrape out of the peel and mash
through a colander. For three pies: Take five eggs, 1½
cups of sugar, 12 tablespoonfuls of pumpkin, a quart of
milk, season with ginger, cinnamon and nutmeg, add a little
salt. MRS. B. F. WHEELER.

PUMPKIN PIE.—Boil tender and strain through a colander. Take two tablespoonfuls of pumpkin, ⅔ of a pint of
milk, one egg, two tablespoonfuls of sugar, and a little
ginger. One pie. MRS. WM. BUCHTEL.

PUDDINGS, SAUCES AND DESSERTS.

DEARBORN PUDDING.—One cup of suet chopped fine,
one cup chopped raisins, one cut sweet milk, ½ cup molasses,
½ teaspoonful cinnamon, pinch salt, one egg, two heaping
teaspoonfuls baking powder sifted with the flour, use flour
enough to make as thick as cake dough. Steam three
hours and serve with a sauce. MRS. WM. ROTHROCK.

DELMONICO PUDDING—One quart milk, three tablespoonfuls corn starch. Mix the starch with water and stir
into the boiling milk. Mix six tablespoonfuls of sugar with
the yolks of five eggs and pour into the starch. Put into a
pudding dish and bake. Beat whites of five eggs with six
tablespoonfuls of sugar and flavor with vanilla; drop with a
spoon on the pudding and brown slightly in the oven.
JENNIE PHILLIPS.

CHERRY PUDDING.—One tablespoonful of sugar, one
tablespoonful of butter stirred together. Then add two
eggs, ⅔ cup of milk and two teaspoonfuls of baking powder,
stir in flour to a thick batter, grease tin, put in a layer of
dough, then a layer of cherries, then sugar and so on until
the tin is full, always leave dough on top. To be eaten with
milk and sugar. MRS. THOS. HAYES.

✳✳   ✳✳   ✳✳   ✳✳   ✳✳

✳✳   ✳✳   ✳✳   ✳✳   ✳✳

COTTAGE PUDDING.--One egg, ½ cup sweet milk, ½ cup of soda, 1½ cup of flour, ½ tablespoonful of butter, ½ tea-. spoonful of soda, ⅛ teaspoonful of salt, beat the butter and sugar and stir in the yolk of the egg.

SAUCE FOR ALL KINDS OF PUDDINGS.--One pint of boiling water; one egg, three spoonfuls of sugar, two spoonfuls of flour.   MRS. A. H. JOHNSTON.

ORANGE PUDDING.--Pare six nice oranges and cut in small pieces into a deep dish with their juice, sprinkling sugar over them. Then take one pint of sweet milk, one tablespoonful of corn starch, the yolks of two eggs, three tablespoonfuls of sugar and thicken the milk, boiling it well and pour over the oranges. When cool, beat to a stiff froth the whites of two eggs, and frost it and brown in the oven.
                    MRS. J. H. HILBISH.

ORANGE PUDDING.--One cup sugar, one tablespoonful flour, one quart milk, yolks of three eggs, reserving the whites, a little salt, make into a custard and let it get cold, peel and slice in small pieces six oranges in a dish and when the custard is cold pour it over the oranges. Then one pint of whipped cream and then the whites which have been beaten slightly sweetened. Brown the frosting and serve cold.   MRS. A. P. BALDWIN.

MOUNTAIN DEW.--Three tablespoonfuls cocoanut, ½ cup cracker crumbs, one cup milk, ½ cup sugar, yolks of two eggs; bake and frost with whites of two eggs and ½ cup of sugar.   MRS. B. C. HERRICK.

COTTAGE PUDDING.--One egg, one cup of sugar, butter size of a walnut, ½ cup of milk, 1½ cups of flour, two teaspoonfuls of baking powder. Bake in oven.

SAUCE.--One cup of sugar, one egg, one cup of boiling water, flavor to suit the taste, rub sugar and egg to a cream, then add the water.   MRS. GROVE BOWERS.

BREAD PUDDING.--Soak bread three hours. Place in a napkin, press out the water. Take one cup of this bread and pick it light with a fork, add one egg and one cup of milk, bake a light brown; make a sweet sauce for it or you can add sugar to your taste.   MRS. IRA MILLER.

SAUCE.—One cup sugar, two eggs without whites, butter size of an egg; beat together and set in a pan of hot water, add ½ cup of cream, set off and add whites of eggs beaten. MRS. JACOB WISE.

TAPIOCA PUDDING.—One cupful of tapioca soaked over night in a pint of water, in the morning add one quart of milk, stirring gently and boil about 20 minutes, then add the yolks of four eggs well beaten, one teacupful of sugar, a little butter, and allow to boil a few minutes longer; flavor with a teaspoonful of vanilla and pour into a dish, cover with the whites of the four eggs beaten stiff and four tablespoonfuls of powdered sugar, serve cold.

MARY PIKE.

TAPIOCA CREAM.—One quart of milk, let it come to a boil, yolks three eggs, three tablespoonfuls of sugar, pinch of salt, ½ teacupful of tapioca soaked in milk. Put in the boiling milk and let stand till it thickens. Take the whites of the eggs, beaten to a stiff froth and cook in steam and when the pudding is slightly cooled drop in.

MISS BROOKS.

DELICATE PUDDING.—Four eggs, yolks beaten separately, add ½ teaspoonful of sugar, two tablespoonfuls of flour and beat until very light and then add a little salt, stir into this gradually one quart of rich hot milk, beat the whites of the eggs to a stiff froth, and stir in the last, flavor with any desirable extract, bake in a quick oven ½ hour. Serve with whipped cream. MRS. GEO. W. PLUMER.

BAKED PUDDING.—One cup of finely chopped suet, one cup flour, sugar, raisins, currants, bread crumbs and sweet milk, two eggs and ½ teaspoonful of baking powder. Serve with sweet cream. MINNIE BAKER.

STEAMED PUDDING.—One cup molasses, one cup milk, one cup suet, one cup raisins, three cups flour, one tea spoonful soda, one teaspoonful cloves, steam one hour.

SAUCE.—One pint water, ¼ cup butter, juice of one lemon, teaspoonful of flour. MRS. J. H. STEESE.

Lesson in Arithmetic. See?

Let us have a talk with you. **YOU** we mean.

Now we do not desire to interfere with any right you may have in this world to do just exactly as you please, as long as doing so does not interfere with the rights of others, but we do want to prove to you by simple, plain, unanswerable arithmetic that you—You we mean—are not doing exactly the square thing by yourself or your family in living in and paying rent for a house. See?

We would like to see every family in Akron safely sheltered under their own roof, and at the risk of making you mad—You we mean—we are going to tell you—You we mean—how you can attain that end, and become the owner of a new $1,400 property. In twelve years' time it will be worth from $2,500 to $3,000 by the payment of but little more in a given time than you are now paying out for the $1,000 property you live in at the rent rate of $12 per month. See?

Call your ten-year-old son or daughter, find him or her a place on your knee, ask the question, "How much do I pay out in rent for one year for this old ranch at $12 per month?" and quick as thought will come the reply "One hundred and forty-four dollars, papa." See? Pursue your inquiry a little futher and ask, "How much would that amount to in twelve years?" and the little one may possibly ask for a slate and pencil, but at the end, as sure as fate will come the answer, "Why papa, it sums away up to seventeen hundred and twenty-eight dollars." See?

Try the same child a little further by asking "What does your papa have for that outlay now?" and see if it does not answer, "I can't figure that because it is all ciphers." Then ask yourself the same question, and when you fail to reach the answer, make inquiries from expert accountants anywhere you may find them, and receive the answer. "Receipts, receipts, all rent receipts." See?

Now, we are honest in saying to you that we would rather see yourself, your wife and children looking on a beautiful home—your own property—instead of rent receipts—nothings at the end of any twelve-year period of your existence and for that reason ask you—You we mean—to pay attention to our proposition and heed our philosophy. See?

Our Proposition. See?

We will sell you a beautiful $1,400 home (we have them from $800 to $2,500, but use the $1,400 home as an illustration) in the Steiner Allotment for, say $200 cash and the balance in $12 per month payments (these payments, which are the same as you are paying in rents for that $1,000 property, including all interest charges) and thus enable you, at the cost of but $200 more than you would have paid in rent for an inferior property, to be the owner of the property you call home at the end of that same twelve-year period, when if you pursue your old course you will have receipts, receipts, all rent receipts. See?

A Little More Arithmetic.

Suppose you confer with your wife on this same subject. Ask her about how much of your hard-earned money has been expended in the way of papering rooms, repairing the pump, laying walks, fixing

[Continued on page 92.]

PRUNE LOAF.—One box of gelatine soaked in a half pint water, one pound best prunes put into water and heated until the pits will easily come out. Chops the prunes fine and crack the pits and chop the kernel very fine; one-fourth pound chopped citron, one cup boiled raisins chopped, a few currants. The juice and rind of two lemons, a little cinnamon and salt. Mix altogether with the dissolved gelatine, then pour over the mixture three pints of boiling water, using the water the prunes were cooked in, two cups granulated sugar, stir well and put in a cold place. Use whipped cream for sauce.

MRS. R. W. SADLER.

PUFF PUDDING.—One cup of sugar, one cup of flour, two teaspoonfuls of baking powder, three eggs, whites and yolks beaten separately, then together. Steam one hour and serve with cream and sugar.

MRS. GEO. W. PLUMER.

TAPIOCA PUDDING.—Teacupful of tapioca, soaked in water over night, quart of milk, three eggs, a little salt, flavor with vanilla. Bake one hour.

MRS. T. N. GANYARD.

TAPIOCA PUDDING.—Soak over night four tablespoonfuls tapioca, three tablespoons cocoanut, one quart milk; thicken with four eggs, and cup of sugar. Cook half an hour. Frosting of whites of the eggs, three tablespoons. sugar, sprinkled with cocoanut.

MRS. S. H. COBURN.

TAPIOCA PUDDING.—Ten tablespoons tapioca, wash in warm water, put in a pan with one quart of milk. Set pan in a kettle of boiling water and stir contents of pan until it thickens, then add two tablespoons of butter and six tablespoons of sugar, flavor to taste, remove whole from the stove, having beaten four eggs very light, stir the eggs in slowly, pour into a well buttered dish, bake three fourths of an hour, serve with cream or custard sauce.

MRS. N. B. STONE.

ENGLISH PLUM PUDDING.—One pound each of raisins, currants, sugar, one pound of beef suet chopped fine, one and one-half pounds bread crumbs, one-fourth of a pound fences, moving from place to place, etc., etc., during your twelve-year payment of $12 per month rents, and see if you do not conclude that it will swell your $1,728 of rent payments up to at least $2,000 or $72 more than your home (your own home, remember) will have cost you in the same time. See?

Figures Do not Lie.

Figures tell the straight cut truth every time, and they always demonstrate the fact that when applied to dollars and real estate they result in homes according to our, and the Building Association plans, and receipts, receipts, all rent receipts according to the plan of the man who lives in a rented house. Now my man—it is you we are talking to—you will please remember that all interest charges are always included in the monthly or weekly payments you make and that you can pay off in full or larger amounts than you agree at any time you desire to do so.

You will always remember that property in Steiner & Co.'s allotment is rapidly and constantly increasing in value, and that as sure as water runs along and through its congenial courses, or grass grows on the fertile grounds of its gentle slopes, just so certain it is that property there at the present price will double in value during the period we have referred to in this, our appeal to you to do your duty toward yourself and family by securing a home.

You ought to own your home. You can own it. If you take our advice you will own it. When you come to think of it seriously, paying rent is frightful. Frightful because it results in nothing but bare shelter and receipts, receipts, all rent receipts, in the end. Open wide your mental eyes. Admit daylight to your intellect. Learn to know that individual ownership of homes is the strong foundation of this republic. Do not theorize, but act. Purchase your home. Purchase it now. Do that which will enable you to say, not many years hence, this is my home. I paid for it with the same money my neighbor used in paying rents. My wife sang all day long within its walls. It was there she gave birth to and nursed our children. It was there I rested after my daily toil was over; every fruit tree, every vine, every shrub, every flower on that lot belongs to me. I love that home, it was the scene of my manhood efforts, and now, in my old age, it is my haven of rest, my refuge.

There is a big difference between 0000 and 2000 when preceded by a dollar mark, although the number of figures is the same. In short, the renter's method results in $0000000 (carry it out as far as you like, it means nothing) and ours, the one we trust you will adopt, results in at least $2,000 in addition to the satisfaction of knowing that you have not lived for naught.

If you fail to see the force of arithmetic as explained to you by that ten-year-old child; if you don't believe the expert accountant or us in regard to this rent-paying business, it would be a good idea to have the following list of rent receipts photographed on your mental, as well as your regular every-day eye vision. The dates on all of them are exactly right. See?

They read exactly like the ones you have been accumulating right along. See?

There is nothing overdrawn about them. See?

Read them it may do you good. See?

[Continued on page 94.]

of citron, six eggs. one nutmeg, cloves and cinnamon to taste. Stir all in new milk, steam before using.

MRS. J. SNYDER.

ENGLISH PLUM PUDDING.—One pound of raisins, one pound of currants, one pound of beef suet chopped fine, one pound of brown sugar, three-fourths of a pound candied citron or orange peel, six cups of rolled crackers, or the same quantity of bread crumbs, six cups of flour, one nutmeg, a little salt, one teaspoonful each of ground cloves, cinnamon and allspice, six eggs, three or four tablespoonfuls of boiled cider; mix the above well, and add enough milk (sweet) to make a thick batter, put it in a pudding cloth and boil constantly five hours, serve with sauce.

SAUCE.—One pint of boiling water, one cup of sugar, a piece of butter the size of an egg, thicken with one tablespoon of corn starch, flavor to taste.

EMMA PICTON.

RICE PUDDING.—Two quarts of sweet milk, one small cup ⅔ full of rice, one cupful blue raisins, five or six tablespoons granulated sugar, enough to make it quite sweet, a little grated nutmeg, a pinch of salt, one tablespoon butter, put all except the raisins in pan to bake, wash the raisins and put them in as soon as it is baking nicely; be sure to use blue raisins and granulated sugar, bake until rice is tender. It will be delicious when cold.

MRS. R. D. NELSON.

SNOW PUDDING.—Three tablespoons of corn starch, two tablespoons of sugar, add a little salt, pour one pint of boiling milk on this and boil two or three minutes, add whites of three eggs beaten stiff.

CUSTARD.—Yolks of three eggs, ½ cup of sugar, ½ teaspoon corn starch, mix and add one pint of milk, boil five minutes, flavor with lemon.

JENNIE MORGAN.

APRICOT FLOAT—Stew half can of apricots soft with a teacupful of sugar and while hot rub through a sieve; when cold beat the whites of three eggs to a stiff froth and add slowly to the fruit, this should be done an hour or two before using. With the three yolks make a custard, boil one

January 1, 1881.—Received from John Renter $12 for rent of house for January, 1881.   A. LANDLORD.

February 1, 1881.—Received from John Renter $12 for rent of house for February, 1881.   A. LANDLORD.

March 1, 1881.—Received from John Renter $12 for rent of house for March, 1881.   A. LANDLORD.

April 1, 1881.—Received from John Renter $12 for rent of house for April, 1881.   A. LANDLORD.

May 1, 1881.—Received from John Renter $12 for rent of house for May, 1881.   A. LANDLORD.

June 1, 1881.—Received from John Renter $12 for rent of house for June, 1881.   A. LANDLORD.

July 1, 1881.—Received from John Renter $12 for rent of house for July, 1881.   A. LANDLORD.

August 1, 1881.—Received from John Renter $12 for rent of house for August, 1881.   A. LANDLORD.

September 1, 1881.—Received from John Renter $12 for rent of house for September, 1881.   A. LANDLORD.

October 1, 1881.—Received from John Renter $12 for rent of house for October, 1881.   A. LANDLORD.

November 1, 1881.—Received from John Renter $12 for rent of house for November, 1881.   A. LANDLORD.

December 1, 1881.—Received from John Renter $12 for rent of house for December, 1881.   A. LANDLORD.

January 1, 1882.—Received from John Renter $12 for rent of house for January, 1882.   A. LANDLORD.

February 1, 1882.—Received from John Renter $12 for rent of house for February, 1882.   A. LANDLORD.

March 1, 1882.—Received from John Renter $12 for rent of house for March, 1882.   A. LANDLORD.

April 1, 1882.—Received from John Renter $12 for rent of house for April, 1882.   A. LANDLORD.

May 1, 1882.—Received from John Renter $12 for rent of house for May, 1882.   A. LANDLORD.

June 1, 1882.—Received from John Renter $12 for rent of house for June, 1882.   A. LANDLORD.

July 1, 1882.—Received from John Renter $12 for rent of house for July, 1882.   A. LANDLORD.

August 1, 1882. Received from John Renter $12 for rent of house for August, 1882.   A. LANDLORD.

September 1, 1882.—Received from John Renter $12 for rent of house for September, 1882.   A. LANDLORD.

October 1, 1882.—Received from John Renter $12 for rent of house for October, 1882.   A. LANDLORD.

November 1, 1882.—Received from John Renter $12 for rent of house for November, 1882.   A. LANDLORD.

December 1, 1882.—Received from John Renter $12 for rent of house for December, 1882.   A. LANDLORD.

January 1, 1883.—Received from John Renter $12 for rent of house for January, 1883.   A. LANDLORD.

February 1, 1883.—Received from John Renter $12 for rent of house for February, 1883.   A. LANDLORD.

March 1, 1883.—Received from John Renter $12 for rent of house for March, 1883.   A. LANDLORD.

[Continued on page 96.]

pint of milk and add a little salt, two tablespoonfuls of sugar and flavoring, dissolve one teaspoonful of corn starch and add, let it boil, and add the beaten yolks, set away to get very cold. Pile the fruit mixture in a dish and pour the custard around it.

MRS. CORNELIUS A. STANLEY.

ORANGE DESERT.—Three oranges, pared and cut in squares. Line a dish with them and pour almost a cup of sugar over this. Make a thin cornstarch of one pint milk, three eggs beaten separately, add a little sugar, and ½ tablespoonful of cornstarch. Stir in the whites just before removing from the fire and pour over the oranges and sugar. To be eaten cold without cream.

MRS. D. WATTER.

SPANISH CREAM.—One pint milk, † package gelatine soaked half an hour in the milk, then put in a kettle and stir while cooking. Three eggs, beat the whites to a stiff froth. put yolks into one cup of sugar and stir into hot milk. Add the whites, flavor with vanilla. Set on ice.

MRS. H. J. SHREFFLER.

ORANGE SHORT CAKE.—One pint flour, teaspoon baking powder, butter size of a walnut; mix with sweet milk. Bake, and when done take off top and place oranges, which have been sliced and sprinkled with sugar for a few hours, between crusts. Serve with whipped cream and powdered sugar.

MRS. B. C. MERRICK.

STRAWBERRY SHORT CAKE.—One egg. ½ cup of milk, one spoonful of shortening, two cups of flour, one cup of sugar. Bake in jelly tins, then put berries between.

PRUNE PUFF.—Three-quarters pound prunes. Cook slowly until soft, then cut in small pieces; one tablespoonful of pulverized sugar. Whites of four eggs beaten to a stiff froth. Stir all together and bake 15 minutes. Watch closely while baking. To be eaten with whipped cream dressing.

MRS. R. W. SADLER.

April 1, 1883.—Received from John Renter $12 for rent of house for April, 1883.   A. LANDLORD.

May 1, 1883.—Received from John Renter $12 for rent of house for May, 1883.   A. LANDLORD.

June 1, 1883.—Received from John Renter $12 for rent of house for June, 1883.   A. LANDLORD.

July 1, 1883. - Received from John Renter $12 for rent of house for July, 1883.   A. LANDLORD.

August 1, 1883.—Received from John Renter $12 for rent of house for August, 1883.   A. LANDLORD.

September 1, 1883.—Received from John Renter $12 for rent of house for September, 1883.   A. LANDLORD.

October 1, 1883.—Received from John Renter $12 for rent of house for October, 1883.   A. LANDLORD.

November 1, 1883.—Received from John Renter $12 for rent of house for November, 1883.   A. LANDLORD.

December 1, 1883. Received from John Renter $12 for rent of house for December, 1883.   A. LANDLORD.

January 1, 1884.—Received from John Renter $12 for rent of house for January, 1884.   A. LANDLORD.

February 1, 1884. Received from John Renter $12 for rent of house for February, 1884.   A. LANDLORD.

March 1, 1884.—Received from John Renter $12 for rent of house for March, 1884.   A. LANDLORD.

April 1, 1884.—Received from John Renter $12 for rent of house for April, 1884.   A. LANDLORD.

May 1, 1884. - Received from John Renter $12 for rent of house for May, 1884.   A. LANDLORD.

June 1, 1884.—Received from John Renter $12 for rent of house for June, 1884.   A. LANDLORD.

July 1, 1884.—Received from John Renter $12 for rent of house for July, 1884.   A. LANDLORD.

August 1, 1884.—Received from John Renter $12 for rent of house for August, 1884.   A. LANDLORD.

September 1, 1884.—Received from John Renter $12 for rent of house for September, 1884.   A. LANDLORD.

October 1, 1884. —Received from John Renter $12 for rent of house for October, 1884.   A. LANDLORD.

November 1, 1884.—Received from John Renter $12 for rent of house for November, 1884.   A. LANDLORD.

December 1, 1884.—Received from John Renter $12 for rent of house for December, 1884.   A. LANDLORD.

January 1, 1885.—Received from John Renter $12 for rent of house for January, 1885.   A. LANDLORD.

February 1, 1885.—Received from John Renter $12 for rent of house for February, 1885.   A. LANDLORD.

March 1, 1885.—Received from John Renter $12 for rent of house for March 1885.   A. LANDLORD.

April 1, 1885.—Received of John Renter $12 for rent of house for April 1885.   A. LANDLORD.

May 1, 1885. - Received of John Renter $12 for rent of house for May, 1885.   A. LANDLORD.

June 1, 1885.—Received from John Renter $12 for rent of house for June, 1895.   A. LANDLORD.

[Continued on page 98.]

CAKES.

CREAM CAKE.—One cup sugar, five tablespoonfuls melted butter. break one egg in a cup and fill up with cold water, two tablespoonfuls of baking powder, two cups flour. Cream for the above. One cup cream, ½ cup sugar beaten together

MRS. THOS. HAYES.

CREAM CAKE.—One cup sour cream, one cup sugar, whites of two eggs, one tablespoonful of butter, ½ tablespoonful soda.

MRS. T. N. GANYARD.

COFFEE CAKE.—One cup brown sugar; one cup molasses, one cup butter. one cup strong coffee, cold, three eggs, 4¼ cups of flour. one cup raisins, chopped, a little citron, one teaspoon soda, a little spice of all kinds.

COFFEE CAKE.—One cup brown sugar, one cup molasses, half cup butter, one cup strong coffee, one egg, four cups flour, heaping teaspoonful soda in flour; melt butter and beat with sugar. add egg. spices, molasses, coffee and flour. Bake in layers, put together with figs in frosting.

MRS. J. R. MELL.

ALMOND CAKE.—Two small cups coffee sugar, six tablespoons melted butter, five eggs, ½ cup sweet milk. two tablespoonfuls baking powder, two cups flour. ½ pound shelled almonds. Stir the butter and sugar to a cream, to which add the yolks beaten to a froth, then the milk. Mix the baking powder with the flour, and add; lastly add the beaten whites. Bake in layers.

FILLING.—Blanch ½ pound shelled almonds. After reserving a handful for top of cake, pound the rest in a mortar with a few drops of rose-water, add the pounded almonds to a frosting which has been flavored with vanilla, spread between the layers. Ice the top of the cake, and strew the reserved almonds over it.

MRS. CORNELIUS JOHNSTON.

AMBROSIA CAKE.—One cup of butter beat to a cream, two of sugar, and whites of seven eggs. one cup of sweet milk, 2½ cups of flour. one cup of cornstarch; ½ teaspoonful

July 1, 1885.—Received from John Renter $12 for rent of house for July, 1885.   A. LANDLORD.

August 1. 1885.—Received from John Renter $12 for rent of house for August, 1885.   A. LANDLORD.

September 1, 1885.—Received of John Renter $12 for rent of house for September, 1885.   A. LANDLORD.

October 1, 1885.—Received from John Renter $12 for rent of house for October, 1885.   A. LANDLORD.

November 1, 1885.—Received from John Renter $12 for rent of house for November, 1885.   A. LANDLORD.

December 1, 1885.—Received from John Reuter $12 for rent of house for December, 1885.   A. LANDLORD.

January 1, 1886.—Received from John Renter $12 for rent of house for January, 1886.   A. LANDLORD.

February 1, 1886.—Received from John Renter $12 for rent of house for February, 1886.   A. LANDLORD.

March 1, 1886.—Received from John Renter $12 for rent of house for March, 1886.   A. LANDLORD.

April 1, 1886.—Received from John Renter $12 for rent of house for April, 1886.   A. LANDLORD.

May 1, 1886. Received from John Renter $12 for rent of house for May, 1886.   A. LANDLORD.

June 1, 1886.—Received from John Renter $12 for rent of house for June, 1886.   A. LANDLORD.

July 1, 1886.—Received from John Reuter $12 for rent of house for July, 1885.   A. LANDLORD.

August 1, 1886.—Received from John Renter $12 for rent of house for August, 1886.   A. LANDLORD.

September 1, 1886.—Received from John Renter $12 for rent of house for September, 1886.   A. LANDLORD.

October 1, 1886.—Received from John Renter $12 for rent of house for October, 1886.   A. LANDLORD.

November 1, 1886.—Received from John Renter $12 for rent of house for November, 1886.   A. LANDLORD.

December 1, 1886.—Received from John Renter $12 for rent of house for December, 1886.   A. LANDLORD.

January 1, 1887.—Received from John Renter $12 for rent of house for January, 1887.   A. LANDLORD.

February 1, 1887. Received from John Renter $12 for rent of house for February, 1887.   A. LANDLORD.

March 1, 1887.—Received from John Renter $12 for rent of house for March, 1887.   A. LANDLORD.

April 1, 1887.—Received from John Renter $12 for rent of house for April, 1887.   A. LANDLORD.

May 1, 1887.—Received from John Renter $12 for rent of house for May, 1887.   A. LANDLORD.

June 1, 1887.—Received from John Renter $12 for rent of house for June. 1887.   A. LANDLORD.

July 1, 1887.—Received from John Renter $12 for rent of house for July, 1887.   A. LANDLORD.

August 1, 1887.—Received from John Renter $12 for rent of house for August, 1887.   A. LANDLORD.

September 1, 1887.—Received from John Renter $12 for rent of house for September, 1887.   A. LANDLORD.

[Continued on page 100.]

of soda; and one teaspoonful cream tartar, or two teaspoons of baking powder. Bake in jelly cake pans. When cold spread with filling made of pint of cream, the whites of two eggs well beaten, one grated cocoanut, the pulp of two oranges well squeezed out, and the juice of one lemon. Then thicken with pulverized sugar.

MRS. D. A. YOUMANS.

APPLE FRUIT CAKE.—One cup of butter, two cups of sugar, one cup of milk, two eggs, one nutmeg, one spoonful cinnamon, and flavoring of all kinds, one teaspoon of soda, $3\frac{1}{2}$ cups of flour, two cups of raisins, $\frac{1}{2}$ pound of citron, $\frac{1}{4}$ pound of figs chopped fine, and three cups of dried apples, soaked over night, chopped fine and stewed two hours in two cups of molasses; beat butter and sugar together, then add milk, in which dissolve the soda, then the beaten eggs and flour, lastly the raisins and apples well stirred in. Pour in a pan and bake for an hour and a half. This is most excellent.

MRS. M. ROGERS.

CONFECTIONERY CAKE.—White part. One cup of butter, cup of sugar, cup of sweet milk, three eggs, three cups of flour, two teaspoons baking powder. Dark part: Half a cup of butter, cup brown sugar, half cup sweet milk, $1\frac{1}{2}$ cup flour, yolks of five eggs, half a tablespoon cloves, allspice and cinnamon together, half teaspoon nutmeg, $1\frac{1}{2}$ cups chopped raisins, cup of sliced citron. Flavor with vanilla.

SAUCE.—Juice of two lemons, $\frac{2}{3}$ of a cup of sugar, put on the stove and let it boil; thicken to the consistency of thin custard with cornstarch dissolved in a little water; when cold put between the layers. Whites of two eggs for the frosting on top.

MRS. M. CHAPMAN.

CORN STARCH CAKE.—One-half cup butter, $1\frac{1}{2}$ cups of sugar, $1\frac{1}{2}$ cups of flour, $\frac{1}{2}$ cup cornstarch, $\frac{1}{2}$ cup of milk, whites of six eggs, $1\frac{1}{2}$ teaspoons baking powder.

CHOCOLATE CAKE.—Three-fourths of a cup of butter, two cups of sugar, one cup of milk, two cups of flour, one cup of cornstarch, two teaspoonfuls baking powder and whites of seven eggs. Bake in a long, shallow pan.

CHOCOLATE.—One-half cup of milk, butter the size of

October 1, 1887.—Received from John Renter $12 for rent of house for October, 1887.
A. LANDLORD.

November 1, 1887.—Received from John Renter $12 for rent of house for November, 1887.
A. LANDLORD.

December 1, 1887.—Received from John Renter $12 for rent of house for December, 1887.
A. LANDLORD.

January 1, 1888.—Received from John Renter $12 for rent of house for January, 1888.
A. LANDLORD.

February 1, 1888.—Received from John Renter $12 for rent of house for February, 1888.
A. LANDLORD.

March 1, 1888.—Received of John Renter $12 for rent of house for March, 1888.
A. LANDLORD.

April 1, 1888.—Received from John Renter $12 for rent of house for April, 1888.
A. LANDLORD.

May 1, 1888. Received from John Renter $12 for rent of house for May, 1888.
A. LANDLORD.

June 1, 1888.—Received from John Renter $12 for rent of house for June, 1888.
A. LANDLORD.

July 1, 1888.—Received from John Renter $12 for rent of house for July, 1888.
A. LANDLORD.

August 1, 1888.—Received from John Renter $12 for rent of house for August, 1888.
A. LANDLORD.

September 1, 1888.—Received from John Renter $12 for rent of house for September.
A. LANDLORD.

October 1, 1888.—Received from John Renter $12 for rent of house for October, 1888.
A. LANDLORD.

November 1, 1888.—Received from John Renter $12 for rent of house for November, 1888.
A. LANDLORD.

December 1, 1888.—Received from John Renter $12 for rent of house for December, 1888.
A. LANDLORD.

January 1, 1889.—Received from John Renter $12 for rent of house for January 1, 1889.
A. LANDLORD.

February 1, 1889.—Received from John Renter $12 for rent of house for February, 1889.
A. LANDLORD.

March 1, 1889.—Received from John Renter $12 for rent of house for March, 1889.
A. LANDLORD.

April 1, 1889.—Received from John Renter $12 for rent of house for April, 1889.
A. LANDLORD.

May 1, 1889.—Received from John Renter $12 for rent of house for May, 1889.
A. LANDLORD.

June 1, 1889.—Received from John Renter $12 for rent of house for June, 1889.
A. LANDLORD.

July 1, 1889.—Received from John Renter $12 for rent of house for July, 1889.
A. LANDLORD.

August 1, 1889.—Received from John Renter $12 for rent of house for August, 1889.
A. LANDLORD.

September 1, 1889.—Received of John Renter $12 for rent of house for September, 1889.
A. LANDLORD.

October 1, 1889.—Received from John Renter $12 for rent of house for October, 1889.
A. LANDLORD.

November 1, 1889.—Received from John Renter $12 for rent of house for November, 1889.
A. LANDLORD.

December 1, 1889.—Received from John Renter $12 for rent of house for December, 1889.
A. LANDLORD.

[Continued on page 102.]

an egg, a cup of brown sugar, quarter of a pound chocolate. Mix and boil until stiff, then add a tablespoonful of vanilla, spread on the cake and set in the oven till dry.

CHOCOLATE CAKE.--One cup sugar, three tablespoons butter, yolks of two eggs and one whole one, ½ cup of milk, 1½ cups of flour, ½ teaspoon vanilla; two teaspoons baking powder.

FILLING.--One cup of brown sugar, ¼ cup of chocolate, whites of two eggs, ½ cup of milk. Boil until thick; spread between the layers and on top. Bake the cake in three layers.

MRS. R. F. WHEELER.

CHOCOLATE CAKE. Two cups sugar, one cup butter, yolks of five eggs and whites of two, one cup of milk. Thoroughly mix two teaspoonfuls baking powder with 3½ cups of flour while dry. Bake in jelly pans.

FILLING.--Whites of three eggs, 1½ cups of sugar, three tablespoons grated chocolate. Heat together and spread between layers and on top of the cake.

MRS. DR. LYDER.

CREAM PUFFS.--One cup of hot water, ½ cup butter; boil the water and butter together, and stir in a cupful of dry flour while boiling; when cool add three eggs, not beaten, mix well; drop by the tablespoonfuls on buttered tins, bake in a quick oven 25 minutes. This makes fifteen puffs.

CREAM.--One cup milk, ½ cup of sugar, one egg, three tablespoonfuls of flour; beat eggs and sugar together, add the flour, and stir in the milk while boiling; flavor when cool; when the puffs are cool open and fill with cream.

BLACK CHOCOLATE CAKE. --One-half cup chocolate, one cup of butter milk or sour milk, melt chocolate and add milk slowly until all is stirred and hot, then let stand until rest of cake is made, 2½ cups of sugar, one cup of butter, two teaspoonfuls of vanilla, one teaspoonful of soda, 2½ cups of flour, five eggs, put whites separate and add last.

MRS. A. HUBLER.

January 1. 1890. --Received from John Renter $12 for rent of house for January, 1890.   A. LANDLORD.

February 1. 1890.—Received from John Renter $12 for rent of house for February, 1890.   A. LANDLORD.

March 1. 1890.—Received from John Renter $12 for rent of house for March, 1890.   A. LANDLORD.

April 1. 1890.—Received from John Renter $12 for rent of house for April, 1890.   A. LANDLORD.

May 1, 1890.—Received from John Renter $12 for rent of house for May. 1890.   A. LANDLORD.

June 1. 1890.—Received from John Renter $12 for rent of house for June. 1890.   A. LANDLORD.

July 1, 1890.—Received from John Renter $12 for rent of house for July, 1890.   A. LANDLORD.

August 1. 1890.   Received from John Renter $12 for rent of house for August, 1890.   A. LANDLORD.

September 1. 1890.—Received from John Renter $12 for rent of house for September, 1890.   A. LANDLORD.

October 1, 1890.—Received from John Renter $12 for rent of house for October, 1890.   A. LANDLORD.

November 1, 1890.—Received from John Renter $12 for rent of house for November, 1890.   A. LANDLORD.

December 1, 1890.—Received from John Renter $12 for rent of house for December, 1890.   A. LANDLORD.

January 1, 1891. Received from John Renter $12 for rent of house for January, 1891.   A. LANDLORD.

February 1, 1891.—Received from John Renter $12 for rent of house for February, 1891.   A. LANDLORD.

March 1. 1891.—Received from John Renter $12 for rent of house for March, 1891.   A. LANDLORD.

April 1, 1891.—Received from John Renter $12 for rent of house for April, 1891.   A. LANDLORD.

May 1, 1891.—Received from John Renter $12 for rent of house for May, 1891.   A. LANDLORD.

June 1, 1891.—Received from John Renter $12 for rent of house for June, 1891.   A. LANDLORD.

July 1, 1891.—Received from John Renter $12 for rent of house for July, 1891.   A. LANDLORD.

August 1, 1891.—Received from John Renter $12 for rent of house for August, 1891.   A. LANDLORD.

September 1, 1891.—Received from John Renter $12 for rent of house for September, 1891.   A. LANDLORD.

October 1, 1891.—Received from John Renter $12 for rent of house for October, 1891.   A. LANDLORD.

November 1, 1891.—Received from John Renter $12 for rent of house for November, 1891.   A. LANDLORD.

December 1, 1891.—Received from John Renter $12 for rent of house for December, 1891.   A. LANDLORD.

January 1, 1892.—Received from John Renter $12 for rent of house for January, 1892.   A. LANDLORD.

February 1, 1892.—Received from John Renter $12 for rent of house for February, 1892.   A. LANDLORD.

March 1. 1892.—Received from John Renter $12 for rent of house for March. 1892.   A. LANDLORD.

[Continued on page 104.]

SOLID CHOCOLATE CAKE.—One-half cup sugar, ½ cup butter; ½ cup sweet milk, two cups flour, one teaspoon soda, two eggs. For the cream, one cupful of chocolate, ⅜ of a cup of sugar, ½ cup of milk, yolk of one egg, one teaspoon of vanilla, cook like a cream, stir in the cake and bake in a slow oven, making three layers, make white frosting put between layers and on top. MAYME BREWSTER.

CHOCOLATE CAKE.—One and one-half cup sugar, ½ cup butter, ½ cup milk, whites three eggs beaten to a stiff froth, 1½ cup flour, a little more may be added if necessary, two teaspoons baking powder, chocolate filling, one cup sugar, ½ cup grated chocolate, ½ cup milk, one egg, piece of butter size of a walnut, flavor with vanilla, boil till it thickens.

FRUIT CAKE.—One cup butter, two of brown sugar, one of New Orleans molasses, one of sweet milk, three eggs, five cups sifted flour, two teaspoons cream tartar in the flour, two teaspoons soda in the milk, tablespoon cinnamon, one nutmeg, one pound raisins, one of currants, one pound citron (citron may be omitted, and ½ quantity of raisins and currants will do). Put flour in a large crock, mix well with cream of tartar, make a well in center, put in other ingredients; having warmed the butter and molasses a little; mix well together with the hands putting in the fruit last after it has been floured, bake two hours in a moderate oven. This will make two good sized loaves. MISS TODD.

FRUIT CAKE.—One pound of flour, one pound of sugar, ¾ pound of butter, seven eggs, two pounds of raisins, two pounds of currants, one pound of figs, ½ pound of citron, ½ pound of dates, ½ teacup lemon juice, ½ teacup strong coffee, two cups molasses, two cups sour cream, two teaspoons soda, one cloves, two of cinnamon, two of nutmeg, bake in a very slow oven. MRS. B. F. WHEELER.

FRUIT CAKE.—One-half cup butter, one cup sugar, two cups flour, ½ cup sweet milk, two cups raisins, one cup currants, yolk of three eggs, one teaspoon cream tartar, ½ teaspoon soda, one teaspoon cloves, one teaspoon cinnamon, two teaspoons allspice, two teaspoons nutmeg. MRS. ELIAS FRAUNFELTER.

April 1, 1892.—Received from John Renter $12 for rent of house for April, 1892.
                                               A. LANDLORD.

May 1, 1892.—Received from John Renter $12 for rent of house for May, 1892.
                                               A. LANDLORD.

June 1, 1892.—Received from John Renter $12 for rent of house for June, 1892.
                                               A. LANDLORD.

July 1, 1892.—Received from John Renter $12 for rent of house for July, 1892.
                                               A. LANDLORD.

August 1, 1892.—Received from John Renter $12 for rent of house for August, 1892.
                                               A. LANDLORD.

September 1, 1892.—Received from John Renter $12 for rent of house for September, 1892.
                                               A. LANDLORD.

October 1, 1892.—Received from John Renter $12 for rent of house for October, 1892.
                                               A. LANDLORD.

November 1, 1892.—Received from John Renter $12 for rent of house for November, 1892.
                                               A. LANDLORD.

December 1, 1892.—Received from John Renter $12 for rent of house for December, 1892.
                                               A. LANDLORD.

Now you have looked 'em over. What do you think of 'em? You have a lot just like 'em in the corner cupboard, in the trunk, in the dressing bureau in the bed-room and various other places. Suppose you hunt up the entire 144 of them. See? Take 12 of them (that will represent one year you know) run into the meat market, offer them in payment for one pound of tough steak and then listen to the laugh the meat man will give you. See?

Take the same lot to your groceryman or milkman; why the grocery man wouldn't give you the sand he puts in his sugar for them, and the milkman would say the time he used in pumping water into his milk was worth more than the entire 144 rent receipts you had accumulated in 12 years. See?

Take 'em all down to the bank with you and ask for a loan of 14 cents, on the basis of giving the whole bunch as security and the cashier would laugh at you instead. See?

Ask your dearest friend for a loan on them and he would give you the laugh instead. See?

Then go around to your family doctor. Tender him that glorious representation of $1,728 in payment for his services in pulling you through a bad spell of sickness and watch for the look of disgust that will be certain to spread over his philanthropic countenance. Take our word for it, his face will look uglier than yours did while swallowing the most nauseous dose he ever gave you. See?

Oh! Truly and honestly they amount to 0000000 in dollars and cents, utterly useless, entirely worthless, no good on earth only as a reminder of the fact that the same money if properly used in the manner we have told you about would have brought you a home that the friend, groceryman, doctor, milkman, butcher or baker would recognize and honor as something real, tangible and good. Something you could always and at any time realize from.

Call and see us and we will more fully explain to you how you can become your own landlord.

N. R. STEINER & CO.,
233 S. Main St., AKRON, O.

DELICATE CAKE —One cup of sugar, ½ cup of butter, ¼ cup of sweet milk, two cups of flour, whites of four eggs and two teaspoonfuls baking powder flavored with lemon or vanilla.

JENNIE MORGAN.

CREAM SPONGE CAKE.—Two eggs broken in a cup, fill with sweet cream, add one cup of white sugar, one heaping cup of flour, one teaspoonful cream tartar, ½ teaspoonful soda. Lemon.

MRS. DOWNEY.

DATE CAKE.—Two cups sugar, ¾ of a cupful of milk, one cup of butter, four eggs, three cups of flour, three teaspoonfuls baking powder. Seed and cut in halves ½ pound dates. Bake the cake in layers, and put between them, first a soft frosting, then dates.

MRS. KELLER.

DELICATE CAKE.—One pound of pulverized sugar and seven ounces of butter beaten to a cream, one pound sifted flour, ½ of a teacup of sweet milk, add milk and flour alternately, one teaspoonful of soda in the milk, two of cream tartar sifted in the flour, add the whites of 12 eggs beaten to a stiff froth, stir in lightly. Lastly, flavor with lemon and almond.

MRS. A. JACKSON.

ANOTHER. —One cup sugar, ¼ of a cup of butter, half a cup of milk, cup of flour, half a cup of cornstarch, teaspoon of baking powder, whites of three eggs.

MRS. J. F. HOY.

EASTER CAKE.—Four cups white sugar, one cup butter, mix together with your hand; beat the whites of four eggs, cup of sweet milk, three cups flour, two teaspoonfuls cream tartar sifted with flour, teaspoonful soda. Flavor with some kind of essence.

MRS. W. B. DICE.

ENGLISH WALNUT CAKE.—One pound of flour, pound of sugar, pound of seeded raisins, three-fourths pound of butter, cup of thin, sour cream, four eggs, a nutmeg, the grated peel of a lemon, tablespoonful of ground cloves, table-spoonful of saleratus dissolved in a little water or milk one and a half cups of English walnuts, chopped. Have some

pieces of walnuts to put on frosting when soft; flavor to taste. Bake in a dripping pan and cut in squares.

MRS. J. E. WISE.

DELICATE CAKE.—One-half cup of butter, one cup of sugar, one cup of sifted flour, ½ cup of cornstarch, stirred in ½ cup of sweet milk, ½ cup of grated cocoanut, two teaspoonfuls baking powder, and the whites of four eggs to be beaten thoroughly and added last. Bake in one loaf.

MRS. F. MASON.

DELICATE CAKE.— Whites of six eggs, one cup of sweet milk, two cups of sugar, four cupfuls of sifted flour, two-thirds of a cup of butter, two teaspoonfuls of baking powder and flavoring. Stir sugar and butter and cream, then add the beaten yolks, then milk and flavoring, part of the flour. Bake carefully in tins lined with buttered white paper.

MRS. GEO. SCHROCK.

COCOANUT CAKE.—Three cups of sugar, one cup sweet cream, one cup butter, five eggs, one cocoanut, one teaspoonful baking powder.

MRS. J. H. STEESE.

WHITE CAKE.—One cup of sugar, ½ cup of butter, ½ cup of milk, the whites of four eggs, two teaspoonfuls of baking powder, two cups of flour, beat eggs and sugar together.

MARY PIKE.

WHITE CAKE.—One cup butter, two of sugar, one of sweet milk, three of flour, white of five eggs, two teaspoons baking powder. Easy made and very good.

MRS. GEO. BREWSTER.

WHITE MOUNTAIN CAKE.—One cup butter, 2 cups of sugar, one cup of sweet milk, four cups of flour, five eggs, two teaspoons cream tartar, one teaspoon soda, flour and icing.

MRS. E. FRAUNFELTER.

WHITE MOUNTAIN CAKE.—One cup butter, two cups of sugar, one cup sweet milk, one cup cornstarch, two cups flour, whites of eight eggs, one teaspoonful of baking powder. Bake in layers. For icing use the whites of three eggs.

MRS. J. H. STEESE.

WHITE CAKE.—One-half cup of butter, one cup of sugar ½ cup of milk, whites of three eggs, two cups of flour, two teaspoonfuls of baking powder.

MRS. J. H. BILBISH.

WHITE CAKE.—Two cups pulverized sugar, one cup of butter, one cup cornstarch. two cups flour, two teaspoons baking powder stirred in the flour. Flavor with rose.

MRS. GAGE.

WHITE FRUIT CAKE.—Whites of four eggs, 1½ cups of sugar, ½ cup butter, ½ cup of sweet milk, one cup raisins, boiled and stoned, two teaspoons baking powder.

MRS. GAGE.

WHITE FRUIT CAKE.—Whites of seven eggs, one cup of butter. two cups of sugar, one cup of milk, three teaspoonfuls baking powder, 3½ cups of flour, one cup of raisins, boiled soft and left whole. Flavor with lemon.

WHITE MOUNTAIN CAKE.—One cup butter, three cups sugar; mix well together; add ½ cup of sweet milk, ½ teaspoonful of soda, and one teaspoonful cream tartar; put into 3½ cups of flour. with the whites of ten eggs beaten stiff. Flavor with lemon and bake in three cakes; then make an icing of one pound of pulverized sugar, and the whites of three eggs; flavor with vanilla.

MRS. SIMPSON.

WHITE MOUNTAIN CAKE.—One egg. one cup of sugar, four tablespoonfuls melted butter. 1½ cups flour in which a teaspoon of cream tartar has been stirred, and ½ cup of milk in which ½ teaspoon of soda has been dissolved; or use two teaspoons of baking powder.

MRS. W. V. ROOD.

WHITE MOUNTAIN CAKE.—Two cups of sugar, one cup of butter, one of milk, three of flour, whites of six eggs, one teaspoonful of soda, two of cream tartar.

MRS. RIDDLE.

COFFEE CAKE.—One and a half cups sugar. one of molasses. one cup strong coffee, one of butter, one of raisins. ¼ pound citron, one egg, one tablespoonful of all kinds of spices, two teaspoonfuls of baking powder. sifted with flour to thicken.

MRS. THOS. HAYES.

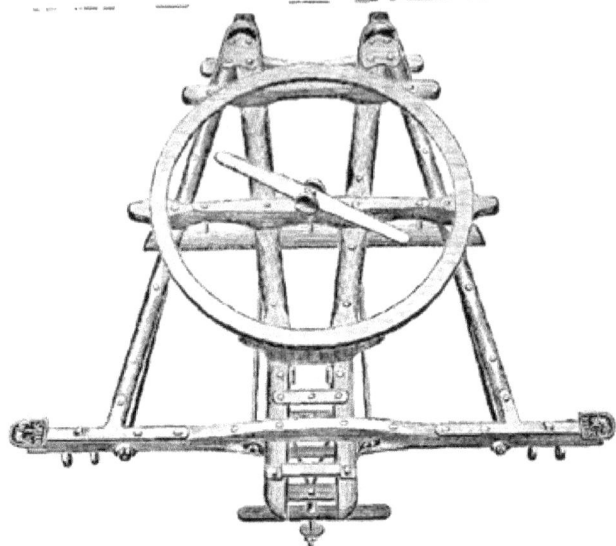

Selle's Platform Giant-Track Gear.

Nos. 40 to 57, for Stiff-Pole and low front wheels to turn under body.
Suited for heavy transfer wagons, ice wagons, brewers' trucks, etc.

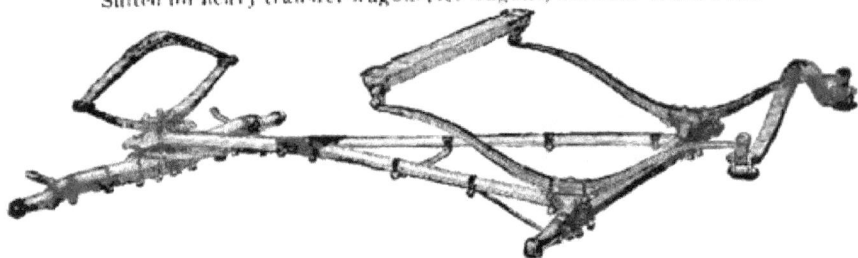

Selle's Half-Platform Gear. Nos. 111, 112, 113 and 114.

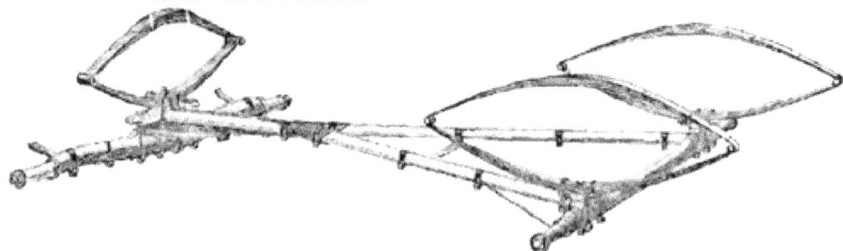

Selle's Three-Spring Gear, Nos. 131, 132, 133 and 134.

If you are looking for the cheapest thing that can be put together and called a wagon—excuse us, we are busy; but if you want good goods at fair prices, come and see us; we can serve you.

THE SELLE GEAR CO., Akron, Ohio.

COFFEE CAKE.—One cup of sugar, one of molasses, one of cold coffee, one of raisins, one of currants, two eggs, ⅔ of a cup of butter, 3½ of flour, large teaspoonful of soda; spice.

MRS. G. W. WEEKS.

CHEAP AND GOOD CAKE.—One cup of sugar, ¼ cup of butter, ¾ cup of cold water, 1¾ cups of flour, whites of two eggs, one teaspoonsful of lemon, two teaspoonfuls of baking powder.

CLARA GALL.

COFFEE CAKE.—One cup of sugar, one of molasses, one of butter, one of cold coffee, one teaspoon soda, one teaspoon of salt.

MRS. E. FRAUNFELTER.

DOLLY VARDEN CAKE.—One cup of sugar, one of milk, one of flour, one egg, three teaspoons baking powder, two tablespoons of butter. Bake two layers of this. Leave enough in the dish for one layer and to it add: One-half cup currants, ½ teaspoonful cinnamon, one teaspoonful all-spice, ½ teaspoonful of cloves. Flavor with lemon.

MRS. LOUIS YERRICK.

SUGAR GINGER BREAD.—One cup butter, two of sugar, ½ cup milk, two eggs, baking powder and a little ginger.

MRS. A. H. JOHNSTON.

GINGER BREAD.—One-half cup butter, one cup light brown sugar, one of molasses, one egg, two teaspoonfuls of ginger, a little nutmeg and flour enough for a moderately stiff batter.

MRS. M. WADDELL.

SOFT GINGER BREAD. One cup molasses, ½ cup sugar, ½ cup shortening, one cup of cold water, ½ teaspoonful of ginger, one of soda and three cups flour.

MRS. F. G. STIPE.

GINGER BREAD.—One-half cup sour milk, ¼ cup butter, one cup molasses, two of flour, one egg, teaspoonful soda. Season to taste.

MOLASSES CAKE.—One egg well beaten, one cup molasses, ½ cup shortening, one teaspoon soda in ½ cup boiling water; the water must be boiling. Stir well, add flour enough to make a thin batter. Cinnamon or ginger, or both as you like.

MRS. MARK HAYNE.

SNOW CAKE.—Whites of ten eggs beaten to a stiff froth, sift lightly on this 1½ cups fine white or pulverized sugar, stir well. and add one cup flour mixed with teaspoon baking powder.   Flavor with lemon or vanilla.

MRS. GEO. BREWSTER.

SNOW CAKE.—One and a half cups of sugar. 1½ of butter. 1½ of flour. 1½ of sweet milk. one teaspoonful of baking powder. whites of four eggs.

CATHERINE TODD.

SNOW BALLS.—Seven small tablespoonfuls butter, one coffee cup of sugar. one pint milk, two teaspoons baking powder. two eggs beaten light,   Flour enough to roll.

MRS. IRA M. MILLER.

WHITE SPONGE CAKE.—Whites of ten eggs beaten to a froth; then add a cup and a third of pulverized sugar, and flavoring: one cup of flour and one teaspoonful of cream tartar.

MRS. N. A. CARTER.

ANGEL CAKE.— Take one cup of flour and put into it one heaping   teaspoonful of Baking Powder, and sift the whole four times.   Beat the whites of eleven eggs to a stiff froth. then beat in 1½ cups of sugar and a teaspoonful of vanilla.   Add the flour and beat lightly but thoroughly. Bake in an ungreased pan slowly, 40 minutes.   When done turn it over to cool, place something under the corner of the pan so that the air will thoroughly circulate underneath and assist the cooling.   Cut it out when cool.

OLD MAIDS' CAKE.—If "old maids" are as good as the new fashioned cake that is named after them, they ought not to remain in single blessedness, but we will give the recipe and let you judge for yourself.

One pound flour, ½ pound sugar, ¼ pound butter or lard, four wine glasses of sweet milk, ½ pound raisins, ¼ pound currants, the same of candied orange peel, ¼ nutmeg grated. two teaspoons ginger, one of cinnamon, one of soda, mix well together and bake slowly for about two hours.

FRUIT CAKE THAT WILL KEEP ONE YEAR.— One pound sugar, one of butter, one of flour, eight eggs, two pounds raisins, one pound currants, ¼ pound citron. one table-

spoonful of molasses, one cupful of sour milk, teaspoon of soda, spices of all kinds. Bake two hours in a moderate oven.

MRS. R. STOCK.

MARBLE CAKE.—Light part. Whites of four eggs, beaten with 1½ cups of white sugar, ½ cup of butter, ½ cup sour milk, 2½ cups flour, soda.

Dark part. Yolks four eggs, one cup brown sugar, ½ cup molasses, ½ cup butter, ½ cup sour milk, 2½ cups flour, soda, spice to taste. One cup raisins makes it still better, can be added or not.

WINNIE McMASTERS.

GOLD AND SILVER CAKE.—Gold. One cup sugar, ¼ cup butter. yolks of eight eggs, ½ cup of milk, 1½ cups flour, a teaspoon baking powder.

Silver. Two cups white sugar, ¾ of cup of butter beaten to a cream, whites of eight eggs, three cups flour, a cup of milk, two teaspoonfuls baking powder.

ANNA C. PRICE.

SILVER CAKE.—Two cups sugar, one butter, whites of three eggs, ½ cup cornstarch dissolved in ½ cup milk, one teaspoonful baking powder, 1¼ cups flour.

MRS. N. D. TIBBALS.

GOLD CAKE.- One cup sugar, ½ butter, yolks of three and one whole egg, ½ cup milk, two cups flour.

MRS. N. D. TIBGALS.

ANGELS' FOOD.--Whites of nine eggs, 1¼ cups granulated sugar, one cup flour, ½ teaspoon cream of tartar and a pinch of salt, separate eggs, add salt and beat half then add cream tartar and beat very stiff, then add sugar, then flour, sifting sugar and flour each five times. Flavor to taste.

MISS SUSIE H. BALDWIN.

LOAF CAKE.—One pint of raised bread dough, one cup of sugar, brown or white, three eggs, one nutmeg grated, one heaping teaspoonful of cinnamon, one heaping teaspoonful of cloves, one large cup of raisins, one heaping teaspoonful of soda worked up the same as bread dough and leave stand an hour then bake; this makes two cakes.

MRS. J. H. WOODS.

COTTAGE PUDDING.

GOLD CAKE.—Yolks of eight eggs, 1¼ cup butter, ½ cup sweet milk, 1½ cups flour, two teaspoonfuls baking powder, cream, butter and sugar, add eggs after they have been thoroughly beaten, then add milk and last the flour and powder. Flavor to taste.

MISS SUSIE H. BALDWIN.

JELLY CAKE.—One cup sugar, one of flour, three eggs, butter the size of an egg, one teaspoonful baking powder sifted in the flour, ½ teaspoonful soda, dissolved in a tablespoonful of milk, bake in jelly cake tins and when cold spread with fruit jelly.

MRS. A. H. JOHNSTON.

JELLY ROLLS.—One cup of sugar, one of flour, three tablespoonfuls boiling water, three teaspoonfuls baking powder, four eggs, pinch of salt.

MAYME BREWSTER.

JELLY CAKE.—Five eggs, one cup sugar, a little nutmeg, one teaspoonful saleratus, two cups sour milk, flour. Beat the eggs, sugar and nutmeg together, dissolve the saleratus in the milk, then stir in flour to make a thin batter like pancakes. Use three or four spoons of the batter to a common round pan. Bake in a quick oven. Three or four of these thin cakes with jelly between, form one cake. Spread the jelly on while the cake is warm.

MRS. CHATFIELD.

MAPLE ICING.—One teacup pure maple syrup boiled until it threads and whipped up with the beaten white of an egg until it thickens, spread over white cake before it begins to harden.

MRS. G. L. A. GALL.

KELLEY ISLAND CAKE.—One cup butter, two sugar, three flour, four eggs, ½ cup milk, 2½ teaspoonfuls baking powder, bake in three jelly cake pans; for filling stir together the grated rind and juice of one lemon, a large grated tart apple, an egg and a cup of sugar, boil four minutes; for frosting, whites of two eggs with sufficient powdered sugar, tablespoonful of lemon juice, ½ teaspoonful vanilla—an excellent cake.

MRS. H. W. BENNETT.

LAYER CAKE.—One cup of milk, 1½ of sugar, two of flour, two eggs, two teaspoonfuls of baking powder, three

tablespoonfuls of butter, take the white of one egg for frosting.

MRS. J. H. DELLENBERGER.

MARBLE CAKE.—For the light part. -One cup of butter, three of white sugar, five of flour (even full), ½ cup of sweet milk, ½ teaspoonful of soda, whites of eight eggs, lemon flavoring.

For the dark part.—One cup of butter, two of brown sugar, one of molasses, one of sour milk, one teaspoonful of soda.

MRS. RICHARD MORGAN.

MARBLE CAKE.-To the whites of five eggs add 1½ cups of white sugar, half cup butter, half cup sweet milk, 2½ cups flour, two teaspoons of baking powder; same quantities for dark part, using brown sugar and spices. This makes two loaves.

MRS. S. L. SEARS.

MAPLE CREAM CAKE.—One and one-half cups sugar, one butter (scant), two flour, three eggs, two teaspoonfuls baking powder, ⅔ cup sweet milk.

Filling—One and one-half cups maple syrup boiled until it can be beaten into a cream.

MATTIE DREWSTER.

PLAIN CAKE.—Three eggs, two cups of sugar, ½ cup of butter, one teaspoonful baking powder, ½ cup sweet milk, ½ teaspoonful soda, flavor with lemon.

SOUR MILK CAKE.—One pint of sour milk, two cups of brown sugar, ½ cup of butter, one tablespoonful of soda, 3½ cups of flour, one cup of raisins, a little salt, cinnamon and cloves to suit the taste.

EMMA PICTON.

SPONGE CAKE.—Three eggs, 1½ cups sugar, one sifted flour, ½ cup water, add another cup flour, two teaspoonfuls baking powder, a pinch of salt—vanilla.

HOME SPICE CAKE.—One cupful of butter, one of cooking molasses, one of sour milk, 1½ of white sugar, two of seeded raisins, four of sifted flour, four well beaten eggs, whites and yolks together, one teaspoonful soda, one of cinnamon, ½ of cloves, three large spoonfuls chopped citron,

GOOD COOKING

nutmeg and salt to taste. Beat butter and sugar together, then stir half of the soda in the molasses to a foam and add to the butter and sugar, then beat remainder of soda, quicken to a foam in the sour milk and add to it the other ingredients, then stir in part of the flour, then eggs, then more flour, then raisins, citron, spices, salt and remainder of flour. This makes two large cakes, or three medium sized, and will keep fresh for several weeks. If baked slowly for one hour will be very nice, though with some stoves may require longer time.

MRS. J. H. ZELLER.

SPICE CAKE.—One cup of molasses, the same of sugar, 2⅔ of butter, one cup of sour milk, three eggs, one tablespoonful of soda, one of cloves, one of nutmeg, 1½ of cinnamon, and three of flour.

MRS. JOHN BELL.

ANOTHER.—Two eggs, one cup brown sugar, one teaspoonful saleratus, one cup sour milk, teaspoonful each of ground cinnamon and cloves, ⅔ of a cup of butter, and either chopped raisins or currants.

MRS. S. N. GROSS.

SPONGE CAKE.—Two cups sugar, four eggs, ¾ cup of water, 2½ cups flour, 1½ teaspoon baking powder.

MRS. D. W. HOLLOWAY.

SPONGE CAKE,—Three eggs, one cup sugar, one of flour, one teaspoonful baking powder; to be baked in two layers.

KATE E. SPERARD.

SPONGE CAKE.—To three well-beaten eggs, add one cup white sugar, and thoroughly stir them together. Then take one heaping cupful of flour and thoroughly mix with it while dry, two teaspoonfuls baking powder. Then stir the flour so prepared into the eggs and sugar, and last of all stir into the whole one tablespoonful hot water. Salt and flavor to taste. Bake immediately.

ANOTHER.—One cup white sugar, one of flour, three eggs, three tablespoonfuls sweet milk, three teaspoonfuls baking powder.

MRS. C. SQUIRE.

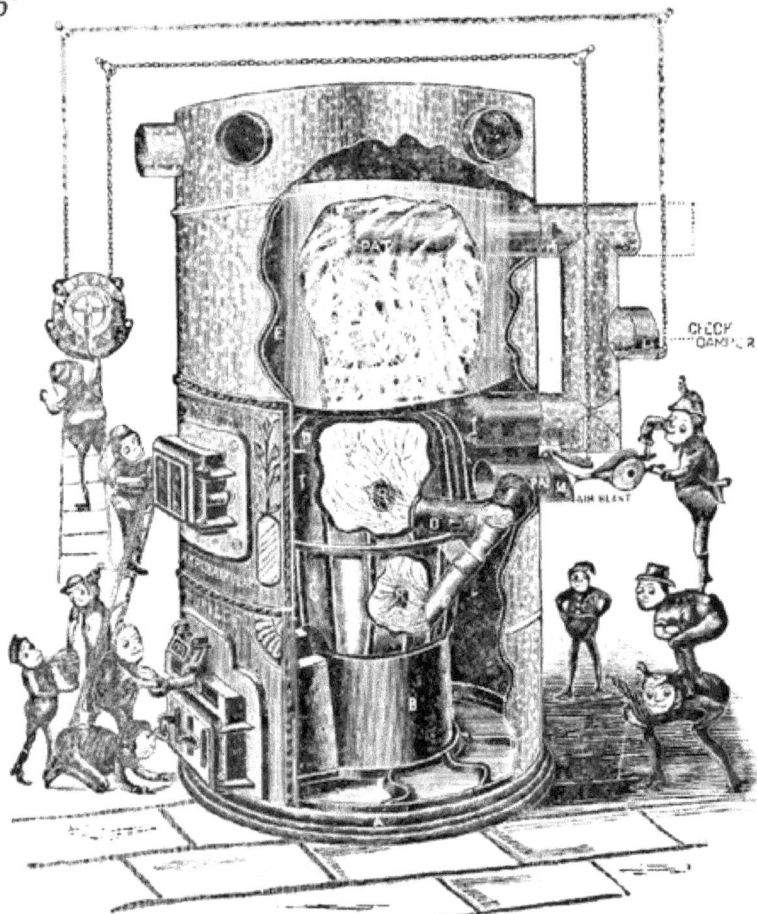

THE AKRON AIR BLAST FURNACE

MNF'D BY

MAY & FIEBEGER AKRON, OHIO. U.S.A.

1314 Akron Air Blast Furnaces are Now in Use.

Every purchaser pleased with their well heated houses and the economy of fuel, ease of management, cleanliness, and many other good features of their Furnaces.

When you are building or remodeling your house, get our price on the cost of a Furnace for your house. Don't fail to examine its many merits.

MAY & FIEBEGER, 114 & 116 N. Howard St., AKRON, O.

ANOTHER.—One pound sugar, ¾ pound of flour, twelve eggs, vanilla and lemon.

MRS. DOWNEY.

GOOD SPONGE CAKE.—Two cups sugar, six eggs, leaving out the whites of three, one cup boiling hot water, 2½ of flour, one tablespoon baking powder in the flour; beat the yolks a little, add the sugar, beat about ten or fifteen minutes; add the beaten whites and the cup of boiling water just before the flour. Flavor with a teaspoon of lemon, and bake in three layers, putting between them icing made by adding to the whites reserved, beaten to a stiff froth, six dessert spoons of pulverized sugar to each egg. Flavor with lemon.

MRS. M. E. ROGERS.

TEA CAKE.—One and a half cups of white sugar, ½ cup butter, ⅔ cup milk, three eggs, two cups flour, one teaspoon soda, two teaspoons cream tartar. Flavoring. Mix; beat the sugar and butter to a cream, then add the egg, well beaten; then the flour, into which the baking powder has been sifted, then the milk, and last the flavoring. Bake quickly.

MRS. A. H. JOHNSTON.

HICKORY NUT CUSTARD CAKE.—Cream, one pound of sugar and half pound butter, add five eggs, beaten separately, one cup sweet milk, one pound flour, three teaspoons baking powder. Flavor with lemon and bake in jelly pans.

CUSTARD.—Place one pint milk in a tin pail and set in boiling water, add a teaspoonful of corn starch dissolved in a little milk, two eggs, ½ cup sugar, two cups of chopped hickory nuts well mixed together to the boiling milk, stir and put between the layers of the cake while both cake and custard are warm.

MRS. LOUIS YERRICK.

ORANGE CAKE.—Half a cupful butter, 1½ of sugar, two of flour, ½ cup milk, three eggs, two teaspoons baking powder, and the juice of one orange. Sift the baking powder well into the flour, cream the butter and sugar; add the milk, the flour, the well beaten egg and the orange juice. Bake in layers and put together with icing, and very thin slices of orange.

MRS. MARY PIKE.

PORK CAKE. One pound salt pork, one of brown sugar, one of French currants, one of raisins, one of citron, one cup molasses, one pint hot water, spices, one tablespoon soda, eight cups flour. Bake two hours.

MRS. MORGAN.

ORANGE CAKE.—Two cups sugar, ½ cup butter, (small) two of flour, ½ cup sweet milk, five eggs, two teaspoonfuls baking powder, juice and grated rind of one orange in the cake.

MRS. DOWNEY.

PORK CAKE.—One pound of pork, one pint of sweet milk, one cup molasses, two of sugar, seven of flour, 1½ teaspoons soda; citron, raisins and cloves. Scald the milk and pour over the pork.

MRS. N. A. CARTER.

COOKIES.

GINGER COOKIES.—One cup of brown sugar, two of Orleans molasses, one of lard, one tablespoon ginger, five teaspoons soda, one cup boiling water. Mix stiff, let raise ten minutes, then roll thin, cut, and bake in a hot oven. These are excellent.

MRS. LOTTIE BREWSTER.

GINGER COOKIES.—One cup New Orleans molasses, one of brown sugar, one of butter and lard mixed, three eggs, three tablespoons cold water, one teaspoon of soda, two of ginger, flour to make stiff enough to roll, but handle soft as possible.

MRS. W. A. PARDEE.

MOLASSES COOKIES.—One cup brown sugar, one of molasses, one of lard, one egg, ¼ cup water, pinch of salt and dessert spoonful of soda.

GINGER SNAPS.—Two cups molasses, one teaspoonful ginger, one cup sugar, one shortening, three teaspoonfuls soda in a little hot water. Mix stiff with flour.

MRS. H. SCHUBERT.

GINGER SNAPS.—One pint of molasses, one cup of butter and lard mixed, one tablespoon of soda, one of salt and ¼ cup ginger in a little hot water.

MRS. E. FRAUNFELTER.

COOKIES.—One cup butter, 1½ cups granulated sugar, seven eighths cup of sour milk; one egg, ½ teaspoonful soda, nutmeg and salt to taste; beat butter and sugar together, add nutmeg and salt, then the beaten eggs and the sour milk stirred to a light foam with the soda, then quickly thicken with flour to a consistency to roll with perfect ease.

MRS. J. H. ZELLER.

COOKIES.—Three eggs, 1½ cups sugar, one cup shortening, one teaspoonful soda, one tablespoonful vinegar, flour to mix stiff, roll thin and bake in a quick oven.

MRS. IDA REX.

COOKIES.—Four eggs; one cup sugar, one butter, teaspoonful soda.

MRS. J. H. STEESE.

COOKIES.—Two eggs, two cups sugar, one cup sour cream, ¼ cup butter, ½ teaspoonful soda, one tablespoonful vanilla, just flour enough to roll.

MRS. LOTTIE BREWSTER.

SUGAR COOKIES.—Four eggs, two cups sugar, 1 butter, one teaspoon soda in a little hot water.

MRS. E. FRAUNFELTER.

GINGER COOKIES.—One teacup molasses, one sugar, one lard, tablespoonful ginger, teaspoonful saleratus in half teacup boiling water, roll thin and bake in a quick oven.

MRS. WM. ROOK.

SPOON CRULLERS—Two tablespoonfuls each of lard, sugar and milk, two eggs well beaten, one teaspoonful baking powder, flour enough to roll out, fry in hot lard.

PEN BEAN.

GINGER SNAPS.—One cup butter, cup molasses, cup lard or melted butter, two eggs, one teaspoon ginger, one teaspoon cinnamon, one tablespoon soda, one of vinegar, a little salt. Dissolve the soda in warm water, add the vinegar to the soda, let it foam well; then add the dough, mix hard, roll thin and bake quick.

MRS. C. G. AUBLE.

O. M. Bietz

Artist in Fresco Painting.

Churches,
Public Buildings
and Private Residences,
Specialties.

If you would see and know my work, go to the Baptist Church on Broadway, the German Lutheran on High Street, the Congregational on High Street, the German Methodist on East Exchange, Main Street M. E. Church on South Main Street, etc.

Res. 134 Glenwood Avenue.

STINGY COOKIES.—Two cups sugar, one lard or butter, one cup cold water, dessertspoonful of soda, mix stiff, roll very thin and bake quickly.

MRS. J. A. LONG.

DOUGHNUTS.—One egg, one cup sugar, one milk, two teaspoonful melted butter, flavoring to taste, three heaping teaspoons baking powder, flour to mold out.

MRS. C. S. FARRAR.

CURRANT COOKIES.—One cup of butter beat to a cream, 2½ cups sugar, three of flour, four tablespoons of cream, three eggs, beat before putting in, one large cup of currants, one teaspoonful vanilla, and three teaspoonfuls baking pow. der, mix well and drop from a spoon on buttered pans; let bake till a good brown.

MRS. D. A. YOUMANS.

COOKIES.—Three cups flour, one of sugar, half a cup of butter, ½ cup water, one egg, two teaspoonfuls baking pow-der, flavoring, sift white sugar over when rolled for cut-ting.

MRS. H. M. SILL.

DOUGHNUTS.—Two quarts of flour, three teaspoonfuls baking powder, ½ cup of sugar, and shortening the size of an egg.

MRS. CHATFIELD.

DOUGHNUTS.—Two cups sugar, three eggs, two cups sour milk, one teaspoonful saleratus, a piece of butter half as large as a hen's egg.

MRS. P. McMILLEN.   .

AUNT MARY ANN KING'S GINGERBREAD.—Four table-spoonfuls of water, three of melted butter, one teaspoonful of ginger, same of soda; put these in a cup, and fill up with . molasses, mix as soft as can be rolled, and bake in a rather slow oven.

SOFT GINGERBREAD.—One quart flour, one cup sugar, one molasses, one butter, one sour milk, two teaspoons soda, three eggs, one tablespoonful of ginger, one teaspoonful cinnamon.

MRS. M. BECK.

GINGER SNAPS.—One and one-half cup molasses, one sugar, one lard, put on and boil not too long, when cool add

one tablespoon vinegar, 1¼ teaspoon soda, three ginger, two cinnamon, one cloves, roll thin and bake.

MRS. D. W. HOLLOWAY.

COOKIES.—Two cups sugar, one egg beaten well, one cup sweet milk, ⅔ cup of butter, ono teaspoon soda, one cream tartar.

MRS. YERRICK.

FRIED CAKES.

"DONUTS."—Two cups milk, two cups sugar, one teaspoon soda, four eggs, seven teaspoons melted lard and butter, a little salt, flour to mix lightly and roll.

MRS. MASON CHAPMAN.

FRIED CAKES.—One cup brown sugar, one sweet milk, one yolk of an egg, one tablespoonful butter, two teaspoonfuls baking powder, pinch of salt.

MRS. LOTTIE BREWSTER.

DOUGHNUTS.—Three tablespoons of melted butter, one cup of soft white sugar rolled, one cup of sweet milk, one large egg (sometimes I use two) well beaten, salt, nutmeg, two teaspoons baking powder, flour enough to make a soft dough, not sticky, yet there is danger of kneading in too much flour, so it sometimes occurs that the last are not so satisfactory as the first. Fry in lard not too hot.

MISS NELLIE ELLIS.

DOUGHNUTS WITHOUT EGGS.—One cup sugar, one cup milk, four tablespoonfuls melted lard, one teaspoon nutmeg, two teaspoonfuls baking powder, a little salt.

MRS. H. SCHUBERT.

FRIED CAKES.—Two eggs well beaten, one large cup of sugar, (a little salt), three tablespoons hot lard, well beaten, one teaspoon soda dissolved in one cup sweet milk, a little cinnamon, two teaspoons cream tartar, 3½ cups flour. Sour milk may be used by omitting the cream tartar.

MRS. T. A. WATTERS.

FROSTING FOR CAKE.—Five tablespoons sweet milk to one cup granulated sugar, boil five minutes, then beat until it is creamy. No eggs.

MRS. ELIZA WEARY.

The Akron General Electric Co.

Desire to call your attention to the desirability and economy of the Electric Light as adapted to the lighting · of STORES, CHURCHES, HALLS AND PRIVATE DWELLINGS.

Reliability of Service,

Cleanliness,

Convenience,

Economy,

Freedom from Odor,

Reduction of Fire Risk,

Purity of Air

Are the accompaniments of Lighting by Electricity.

NO HOME with all these comforts within easy reach CAN AFFORD to be without this Light.

For full particulars regarding cost and dispensation of Electric Light, Heat and Power, you are cordially invited to call at the Company's Office, Cor. West Market and Canal Streets.

Visitors are welcome to inspect the station any day except Sunday, between the hours of 6 and 8 P. M.

SANDWICHES AND OMELETS.

LETTUCE SANDWICHES.—Make a dressing as follows; ½ cup vinegar, ½ cup water, one egg, one teaspoon corn-starch, one teaspoon yellow ground mustard, ¼ teaspoon salt, two tablespoons sugar, cayenne pepper enough to ex-tend ¼ inch up on the point of a teaspoon. Bring water and vinegar to a boil. Meanwhile beat thoroughly together the other ingredients, stir the mixture in the boiling vinegar, let it boil long enough to cook the cornstarch. When cool it is ready for use. Butter thin slices of bread on which lay crisp leaves of lettuce. Spread thinly the dressing. Lay slices together like any sandwich, bringing two pieces of lettuce with each.

MRS. D. D. BENNETT.

LUNCHEON.—Sandwiches, potato salad, cold pork or veal, cream puffs, tarts, fruit, chocolate.

MISS BINNIE LONG.

EGG AND CHEESE SANDWICH.—Grate one cup of mild cheese and mix it with four eggs which have been boiled three minutes, cooled and then chopped fine, season with butter, pepper and salt, and spread on thin slices of brown bread, buttered before it is cut from the loaf; these should be cut small and of any desired shape.

BAKED OMELET.—Boil ½ pint of milk, beat six eggs thoroughly, the yolks and whites separately, put ½ teaspoon of salt, and a piece of butter half as large as an egg, into the beaten eggs, and pour all into a deep dish to bake. It should be a nice brown. Eat hot.

MRS. J. H. STEESE.

CHEESE SANDWICHES.—Into ½ pint of crumbled cheese pour a like quantity of milk, and a piece of butter the size of an egg. Stir over the fire until the cheese dissolves and the whole become a thick paste. Spread between slices of bread.

BREAD OMELET.—One cup milk, one desertspoon but-ter, salt and pepper to taste. Add three well-beaten eggs, fry in butter.

MRS. N. D. TIBBALS.

OMELET.— Six eggs, one cup milk, one tablespoon butter, one tablespoon flour; melt the butter in the milk; beat the yolks with the whites thoroughly; and the milk and the butter, then the whites beaten to a stiff froth, and add a little salt. Cook in a spider on top of the stove and turn very carefully.

BEST WAY OF MIXING MUSTARD.—Four teaspoonfuls best English mustard; two of salt, two of white sugar, one of white pepper, two of salad oil, vinegar to mix to a smooth paste, celery or Tarragon vinegar if you have it, one small garlic minced very small. Put the mustard into a bowl, and wet with the oil, rubbing it in with a silver or wooden spoon until it is absorbed. Wet with vinegar to stiff paste; add salt, pepper, sugar and garlic, and work all together thoroughly, wetting little by little with the vinegar until you can beat it as you do cake-batter. Beat five minutes very hard; put into wide-mouthed bottles—empty French mustard bottles, if you have them—pour a little oil on top, cork tightly, and set away in a cool place. It will be mellow enough for use in a couple of days, and keep a long time.—Common Sense in the Household.

PICKLES.

CUCUMBER PICKLES.—Place two hundred small cucumbers into a stone jar, scald two gallons of vinegar and with the vinegar six tablespoonfuls of salt, a piece of alum size of a walnut, two ounces each of spice, white mustard seed sewed into a bag. Put 1½ dozen red peppers and a large sized horseradish root with the pickles and pour the hot vinegar and spice over them.

MRS. THOS. HAYES.

GREEN TOMATO PICKLES.—One peck green tomatoes, eight onions, four green peppers, one cup sugar, one tablespoonful of pepper, one tablespoonful whole cloves, one tablespoonful mustard, one of mace, slice the tomatoes, peppers and onions, put in layers and sprinkle over them the salt, and let them stand over night. In the morning press

dry through a sieve, put in the spice in a thin muslin bag and cover with vinegar, stew slowly about an hour or until the tomatoes are as soft as you desire (the onions can be omitted if you wish.)

MRS. A. H. JOHNSTON.

FRENCH PICKLES.—One peck green tomatoes sliced and put in weak salt brine over night. In the morning drain well and add eight onions sliced. Put onions and tomatoes in a kettle to heat with one quart of vinegar and a little sugar. For the spices take one tablespoonful cinnamon, ½ teaspoonful cloves, one teaspoon nutmeg, also pepper to suit taste. Tie the spices in a cloth and boil separately, then add the liquid to the pickles.

MRS. H. SCHUBERT.

CHOW CHOW.—One-fourth peck onions, ½ peck tomatoes, five dozen large green cucumbers, pared and sliced. Slice all very fine with a hash knife. Put in a few small cucumbers and four red and green peppers. Sprinkle one pound salt on and let stand over night; then drain. Add ½ ounce of mace, one ounce of mustard seed, one ounce of celery seed, two quarts chopped celery, ½ ounce tunica, ½ ounce whole cloves, three tablespoons ground mustard, two pounds brown sugar, one large root of horse-radish, one gallon good cider vinegar. Boil 20 minutes. Put in jars and seal while hot.

MRS. J. H. STEESE.

CHOW CHOW.—Two quarts green tomatoes, one quart onions, one cauliflower, 20 good-sized cucumbers, two tablespoons brown sugar, ½ tablespoon black pepper, a lump of alum about the size of a hazel nut, two ounces of mustard, ½ tablespoon cinnamon, two quarts vinegar. Chop the tomatoes, onions and cauliflower, and cucumbers and let them stand 24 hours in a good brine, then drain thoroughly, and put everything into the vinegar and boil 20 minutes.

MRS. MARK HAYNE.

TOMATOES PICKLED WHOLE.—Pick tomatoes just commencing to turn red, make a number of incisions with a sharp pointed knife, pack them in a large jar, and cover with a strong salt water, and let them set in a cool place ten days. Then rinse and drain well, have pared and salted onion

(plenty) ready, and lay tomatoes first in the jar, then onions alternate until the jar is near full, and cover with good vinegar cold, and a pound or two of brown sugar, (according to the quantity). In about ten days more, pour off the vinegar and boil with the spices in a large bag down some, and add more strong vinegar if necessary, salt and pour over cold. Spread the spice bag over the top, lay on a plate, set away in a cool place and they will keep nicely for months. They are very delicious.

MRS. ELIZA WEARY.

PICCALILLI.—Half peck each of green tomatoes, onions, green cucumbers, and green peppers, half a head large cabbage; chop separately, then mix them and sprinkle over them one teacup of salt; let drain in a basket 24 hours; then cover with vinegar and set on the stove till it comes to a boil. Drain for three days; turn on hot vinegar in which are three tablespoons ground cinnamon, a grated nutmeg and two tablespoons white mustard seed.

MRS. A. JACKSON.

ANOTHER.— One peck tomatoes, three heads of cabbage, six onions, three red peppers. Syrup: Three quarts vinegar, two pounds sugar, two tablespoons mustard seed, chop tomatoes fine; soak in salt and water 24 hours; chop cabbage fine and mix, scald both in weak cider vinegar, let it stand 24 hours, then drain, chop onions and peppers, add mustard seed and mix thoroughly with the tomatoes and cabbage scald in the syrup; put into cans and seal tight. Chopped celery may be added if liked.

MRS. E. L. SIMPSON.

PICCALILLI.—One bushel green tomatoes, ½ dozen green peppers, 12 onions chopped fine, one teacupful grated horse radish, one cup ground mustard seed, ½ dozen whole cloves, ½ ounce ground cinnamon, cabbage and celery added to suit taste, sprinkle the chopped article with salt and stand over night, drain, add vinegar enough to moisten and scald until tender, drain again, add spices (mixed), pack in jars and cover with scalding vinegar.

LILLIAN VITOU.

TOMATO CATSUP. — Five pints stewed tomatoes, one quart vinegar, two tablespoonfuls sugar, two salt, one red pepper, two black pepper, two cinnamon, three mustard

strain tomatoes through a fine sieve, add the spices and cook slowly three hours, then bottle and seal it.

MRS. GROVE BOWERS.

CHILI SAUCE.--Two large onions, four green peppers, chopped fine with the onions, 12 large ripe tomatoes, put them into the kettle with onions and peppers, add two tablespoons salt, the same of brown sugar, four teacups vinegar, boil slowly for two hours then bake.

CANNED STRING BEANS.--Break up the bean pods and fill the can as full as possible, then fill the can with cold water, fasten on the cover. Place the cans in a boiler of water, let the water completely cover the cans, let them boil slowly three hours, remove the cans and tighten the covers again. Put a cloth between and under the cans. Green peas are canned the same way.

CANNED CORN.--Shave the corn from the cob and pack it in glass cans, then seal them tight, place the cans in a boiler of cold water, put cloth between and under the cans, let them boil three hours, the water must completely cover the cans, when the cans are removed, tighten the covers again.

MRS. GROVE BOWERS.

CHOW-CHOW--One peck green tomatoes chopped fine, and drained well; half a dozen green peppers, half a dozen large onions; boil the whole in one quart of vinegar, and drain again; then take one quart of fresh vinegar, a bottle of French mustard, three cups sugar, a tablespoonful of cloves, two of cinnamon, one of salt and one of pepper; boil in this five minutes.

MRS. L. H. HANSCOM.

CHOW-CHOW.--One quart of large cucumbers cut lengthwise, one quart small cucumbers, quart of large green tomatoes sliced, quart small green tomatoes sliced, one large cauliflower, picked in pieces, six green peppers, cut all up and put into salt water 24 hours; then scald in same and strain. For the paste--six tablespoons mustard, one cup of flour, a little vinegar, one tablespoon turmeric, and one cup of sugar; stir into two quarts boiling vinegar, mixing well together.

MRS. M. CHAPMAN.

MIXED PICKLES.—Three hundred small cucumbers, eight good sized green peppers, sliced, one large horse-radish root, two quarts very small white onions, one quart bean pods, cut in pieces. Put the mixtures in a brine, that will bear up an egg, for 24 hours; drain three hours, scald two gallons white vinegar, add ¼ of a pound each of white and black mustard seed, one teaspoonful cayenne pepper, and one ounce turmeric. Pour over the pickles and when cold add a pint bowl of mustard prepared as for the castor. I put the pickles in very cold brine with pieces of ice.

MRS. G. D. BATES.

PICKLED CUCUMBERS.—Soak the cucumbers in strong brine for two days, take out and put in fresh water over night, when soaked put on the back of the stove and cover with vinegar in which you put sugar, in the proportion of one pint of sugar to a quart of vinegar, add one ounce each of allspice, cinnamon and cloves mixed. Let scald on the back of the stove all the forenoon; before tying up put horse-radish and one ounce of mustard seed on top.

MRS. B. F. WHEELER.

TO HARDEN PICKLES AFTER THEY ARE TAKEN OUT OF BRINE. A lump of alum put in the vinegar and horse-radish cut in strips will make them crisp.

MRS. N. A. CARTER.

'PICKLED CUCUMBERS.—Two gallons of vinegar, two ounces each of whole cloves and allspice, two ounces alum, four ounces mustard seed, six tablespoons salt; into a stone jar pack two hundrd small cucumbers, a dozen and a half small red peppers, (vary quantity of peppers to your taste), and a good sized horse-radish root cut in small pieces. Tie the pieces in a bag, scald them with the vinegar thoroughly, and pour over the cucumbers. This method saves the trouble with the brine, and you need not seal them, for they will keep nicely and are always handy.

MRS. W. E. GAYLORD.

WATERMELON PICKLES.—Take off the green and red parts of the rind of a watermelon; cut in pieces about two inches long, put in warm water to nearly cover them, add two heaping teaspoons salt to a gallon of rinds, boil till you can pierce them with a silver fork, drain and dry them on a towel, place them in a jar, and put over them boiling hot syrup. made in proportion of a quart of vinegar to three pints of sugar. Heat the syrup boiling hot the next day and pour over them, the next two days do the same, but scald in vinegar bits of cinnamon and a few cloves. Treat ripe cucumbers in the same manner.

JELLY.

PREPARING FRUITS FOR CANNING.

BOIL MODERATELY	TIME FOR BOILING FRUITS.	SUGAR TO QUART.
Cherries	5 minutes	6 ounces.
Raspberries	6 "	4 "
Blackberries	6 "	6 "
Plums	10 "	8 "
Strawberries	8 "	8 "
Whortleberries	5 "	4 "
Pie Plant, sliced	10 "	10 "
Small sour pears. (whole)	30	8 "
Bartlett pears, in halves	20	6 "
Peaches. in halves	8	4 "
Peaches, whole	15	4 "
Pine Apples, sliced	15	6 "
Crab Apples, whole	25	8 "
Sour Apples, quartered	10 "	6 "
Ripe Currants	6 "	8 "
Wild Grapes	10 "	8 "
Quinces	15 "	8 "
Tomatoes	20 "	10 "

SUGGESTION.—Cross the blades of two steel knives, set your can or jelly glass upon them, pour in the hot fruit or jelly. It is not necessary to heat the cans.

EXPERIENCE.

APPLE JELLY.—Pare, core and cut thirteen good apples into small portions, when cut put them into two quarts of cold water, boil them in this with a peel of a lemon till the substance is extracted, and half the water wasted, drain through a sieve, to a pint of the water add one pound of loaf sugar. pounded, the juice of one lemon, and the whites of two eggs. put into a pan, stir in till it boils, skim till clear and then mold it.

MRS. C. H. GROVER.

LEMON JELLY.--Four lemons, sliced, one pound sugar, one quart boiling water poured over them, dissolve two ounces of gelatine. mix with lemon and sugar and strain into molds.

MRS. N. D. TIBBALS.

APPLE JELLY.--Slice the apples, skins, cores and all put them in a stone jar with small quantity of water to keep them from sticking. then place the jar in water and let them remain boiling until perfectly soft, then strain and to one pint of the liquor add three-quarters of a pound of loaf sugar, boil and clear with the whites of two or three eggs beaten to a froth. When it jellies pour into the glasses to cool and seal them.

QUINCE HONEY.--One pint of water, one pint of sugar, let come to a boil. grate two sour apples and one quince, put into the syrup as fast as grated, cook until it jellies.

MRS. WM. ROOK.

CRAB APPLE JELLY.--Boil the fruit whole in water enough to cover it until perfectly soft, then pour into a coarse linen bag and let it drip until it ceases. then press it a little. Allow one pound of sugar to each pint of juice. If you choose add the juice of a lemon to each quart of syrup, boil the juice first, then skim it. heat the sugar in a dish in the oven and add it as the juice boils up. Boil gently 20 minutes and pour into tumblers.

RAISIN SAUCE.--Raisins soaked over night and next morning stewed till tender, and sweeten just as they are done, makes an economical and palatable sauce for supper.

MRS. B. C. HERRICK.

TOMATO BUTTER.--Take ripe tomatoes boil soft and put through a colander; to eight pound of tomatoes add four pounds brown sugar, two tablespoonfuls each of allspice and cloves, and a little more than that of cinnamon, boil until thick.

ORANGE FLOAT.—One pint milk, three eggs, four tablespoonfuls sugar, heat the milk to near boiling, have the whites beaten and lay on the milk to steam, take out the whites and put in the yolks with the sugar and one teaspoonful cornstarch, pinch of salt, two oranges sliced thin and sprinkled with sugar, pour the mixture over the oranges and put the whites on top.

MRS. O. D. CAPRON.

ELDERBERRY BUTTER.—Take ½ bushel of elderberries, wash, cook and put through a sieve, put them into a porcelain kettle, and boil until quite thick, add ten pounds granulated sugar, two tablespoonfuls cinnamon, one even teaspoonful ground cloves, and one grated lemon, boil until a thick jelly, stirring constantly.

MRS J. M. McCREERY.

CANNING PIE PLANT.—I would like everybody to try this: Cut up your pie plant as for pies, have your glass can or any other by you, fill the can as full as you can get it, then fill up with cold water, and seal up tight. This method saves cooking, sugar and trouble, and is just as nice as when you cut from the plant.

MRS. M. E. ROGERS.

ICES.

PINE APPLE ICE.—One juicy ripe pineapple, peeled and cut small; juice and grated peel of a lemon, one pint of sugar, one pint of water; strew the sugar over the pineapple and let it stand one hour; mash all together and strain out the syrup; add the water and freeze.

MRS. B. C. HERRICK.

LEMON ICE.—One gallon of water and four pounds of white sugar, well boiled and skimmed; when cold add the juice of a dozen lemons and the sliced rind of eight, and let infuse an hour, strain into the freezer without pressing, and stir in the well-beaten whites of twelve eggs.

MRS. E. O. STANLEY.

LEMON ICE CREAM.—One pint of sweet cream, three pints new milk, one pound loaf sugar, and two lemons; boil and stir in gradually. If you have no lemons use four eggs. Put into a freezer and surround the freezer with ice and coarse salt on all sides; while freezing, stir it well, scraping it down from the sides.

VANILLA ICE CREAM.—Boil a vanilla bean in a quart of rich milk until it has imparted the flavor sufficiently, then take it out and mix it with the milk, eight yolks and whites beaten well; let it boil a little longer, make it very sweet, for much of the sugar is lost in the operation of freezing.

STRAWBERRY ICE CREAM is made in the same manner; the strawberries must be very ripe, and the stems picked out. If rich cream can be procured it will be infinitely bet- ter. The custard is intended as a substitute, when cream cannot be had.

COCOANUT ICE CREAM.—Take the nut from the shell, pare it and grate it very fine; mix it with a quart of cream, sweeten and freeze it. If the nut be a small one it will re- quire one and a half to flavor a quart of cream.

CHOCOLATE ICE CREAM.—Scrape a quarter of a pound of chocolate very fine, put it in a quart of milk, boil it till the chocolate is dissolved, stirring it constantly; thicken with six eggs. A vanilla bean boiled with the milk will im- prove it.

PINE APPLE ICE CREAM.—Ingredients: Half a pound of preserved pineapple, one pint of cream, the juice of a small lemon, one gill of raw milk, a quarter of a pound of sugar. Cut the pineapple into small pieces, bruise it in a mortar; add the sugar, lemon juice, cream and milk, mix well together, press through a hair seive, and freeze twenty- five minutes.

IDA FISHER.

PINE APPLE SHERBET.—Take one large pineapple, grate and mix with three quarts of water, one ounce of dis- solved gelatine, four lemons, six eggs, whites, sweeten and freeze.

MAE S. MILLER.

CANDIES.

CREAM CANDY.—The cream; Use the white of one egg and the same quantity of water for one pound of sugar, whip the egg and water together, then add sugar until you cannot add more, knead as bread, use figs, dates or nuts for filling.

MRS. MEACHAM.

BUTTER SCOTCH.—Seven tablespoons molasses, two water. two sugar and two of butter. Boil till it will work easily when dropped into cold water.

No 2.—One cup molasses, one sugar, ½ cup butter, boil as above.

MRS. MEACHAM.

CRULLERS.—One egg, three tablespoons sugar, same of melted butter, mold hard.

MRS. STONE.

HICKORYNUT MACAROONS Four eggs beaten till very light. one pint of sugar, ½ pint of flour, 1½ pints of hickory-nut meats, bake in a moderately hot oven.

MRS. J. F. HOY.

HICKORYNUT DROPS.—One cup of meats, one brown sugar, one egg, one tablespoonful of flour, a big pinch of salt, stir the flour in the sugar, beat thoroughly and slowly into the egg.

MRS. NELLIE M. DODGE.

CREAM COCOANUT CANDY.— One and-one-half pounds sugar, one half cup of milk, boil ten minutes, one grated cocoanut added, boil until thick, put on greased paper quite thick. When partially cold cut in strips.

MRS. H. M. SILL.

CHOCOLATE CARAMELS.—Three cups brown sugar. one cup of milk, ½ cake chocolate, one piece of butter size of an egg, boil until thick, pour in buttered pan and when cool cut in squares.

No. 2.—Two cups molasses, one of brown sugar, one of milk, ½ pound baker's chocolate, a piece of butter size of an egg, beat all together and boil until it thickens in water; turn in well buttered tins, when nearly cold cut into small squares.

MRS. LEWIS MILLER.

SALTED PEANUTS.—Salted peanuts are now taking the place of salted almonds on many of the most fashionable tables. They are blanched, buttered and salted in exactly the same way that the almonds are prepared.

HICKORY NUT DROPS.—One and a half cup sugar, one cup butter, two eggs, one cup nuts (chopped), little soda, flour to roll out thin, frost and put meats on top.

MRS. MASON CHAPMAN.

WHITE CANDY.—One pound sugar, ½ cup water, one teaspoonful vinegar, flavor with lemon or vanilla, boil without stirring until brittle, turn out on buttered plates, when cool, pull until white and cut in squares.

MABLE L. STIPE.

BEVERAGES.

COFFEE.—For thirty persons: To one pound of good coffee, add two eggs beaten with a little cold water, mix well, then pour over ten quarts of boiling water, and steep, not boil, about ten minutes over steam, if you can, when it will be ready to serve. By making it thus, it retains all the oil and fragrance of the fresh ground coffee.

MRS. ELIZA WEARY.

RASPBERRY SHRUB.—Place red raspberries in a stone jar, cover them with good cider vinegar, and let stand over night; next morning strain, and to one pint of juice add one pint of sugar, boil ten minutes, and bottle while hot. One or two teaspoons of this syrup in a glass of cold water makes a delicious summer drink, especially for the sick.

MRS. W. A. PARDEE.

UNFERMENTED GRAPE JUICE.—Take five pounds of Concord grapes picked from the stems and washed. Put into a preserving kettle with one quart of cold water, and let it come to a boil; boil a few minutes, then set it aside to cool, and strain through a fine cheesecloth bag. Return it to the kettle with a pound of granulated sugar, and once more let it reach a boil. Have the bottles heated, pour the grape juice in while boiling hot, and pound the corks in firmly, cutting them off even with the tops of the bottles, and sealing well. This makes a healthful home drink.

MRS. W. A. PARDEE.

WEIGHTS AND MEASURES.

One quart of sifted flour ... 1 pound.
One quart of corn meal ... 1 pound 2 ounces.
One pint of butter closely packed ... 1 pound.
One quart of powdered sugar ... 1 pound 7 ounces.
One quart of granulated sugar ... 1 pound 9 ounces.
A piece of butter the size of an egg ... 2 ounces.
The white of a common sized egg weighs 1 ounce.
Ten eggs are equal to ... 1 pound.
A common sized tumbler holds ... ½ a pint.
A common wine glass holds ... ½ a gill.

LIQUIDS.

Four tablespoonfuls ... ½ a gill.
Eight tablespoonfuls ... 1 gill.
Two gills ... ½ a pint.
Four gills ... 1 pint.
Two pints ... 1 quart.
Four quarts ... 1 gallon.
Four teacups of liquid ... 1 quart.

"Finis coronat opus."

Professional Directory.

PHYSICIANS.

J. O. BALLARD, M. D.,

No. 1121 S. Main St.,

AKRON, O.

O. D. CHILDS, M. D.,

Cor. Market and Broadway,

Telephone 22.   AKRON, O.

J. V. CLEAVER, M. D.,

P. O. Building,

Telephone 319.   AKRON, O.

E. CONN, M. D.,   •

Office Cor. Mill and Howard Sts., Opposite Post Office.

Res. 1104 S. Main St.,   AKRON, O.

C. C. DAVISON,
PHYSICIAN AND SURGEON.
Residence—109 Broad St.
Office—1184 E. Market St.
Office Hours—8 to 12 A. M., 1 to 2 P. M.
and 7 to 9 P. M. Telephone, No. 57.

H. M. FISHER, M. D.,

P. O. Building,

AKRON, O.

A. K. FOUSER, M. D.,   •

Office and Residence, 161½ S. Broadway.

Telephone 246.   AKRON, O.

T. C. PARKS, M. D.,

Office, 706 S. Main St.
Residence, 416 E. Exchange St.

AKRON, O.

C. W. MILLIKEN, M. D.,

Office, 1174 East Market St.,

AKRON, O.

L. M. HOLLOWAY, M. D.,

Office and Residence, 1020 S. Main St.

AKRON, O.

DR. ALBERT HOOVER,

OCULIST AND AURIST,

Akron Savings Bank Bld'g, AKRON,O.

HOURS:—9 to 12 A. M., 2 to 5 P. M., 7 to 8
P. M.

R. M. MURPHY, M. D.,
Specialist in diseases of the Eye, Ear,
Nose and Throat.
ROOM 31, ARCADE,
Permanently Located.   AKRON, O.

C. M. HUMPHREY, M. D.,

Office and Residence, 1013 S. Main St.

AKRON, O.

E. K. HOTTENSTEIN, M. D.,

211 E. Mill Street,
Residence, 126 Carroll St.

Phone 503.   AKRON, O.

PROFESSIONAL DIRECTORY. Physicians.--Concluded.

J. L. SHIREY, M. D.,

Office, 208 E. Market Street.
Residence, 270 W. Market Street.
Telephones:—Office, 323; Residence, 261.

AKRON, O.

F. E. STOAKS, M. D.,

THE ARCADE,

AKRON, O.

L. S. SWEITZER, M. D.,

Residence, 505 E. Market St.

Telephone 534.   AKRON, O.

E. O. LEBERMAN, M. D.,

Office, 111 W. Exchange St.

Residence, 603 Bowery St.

Telephone 514.   AKRON, O.

DENTISTS.

MASON CHAPMAM,

Office, Cor. Mill and Broadway,

Telephone 372.   AKRON, O.

J. W. HILLMAN,

DENTIST,

151 S. Howard St., over Harper's
Drug Store,

AKRON, O.

DR. N. B. SIBLEY'S

ODONTUNDER DENTAL PARLORS,

158 Main St.,   AKRON, O.

W. B. CONNER, D. D. S.,

ARCADE BLOCK,

AKRON, O.

F. W. KNOWLTON, D. D. S.,

DENTAL OFFICE,

217 E. Market St.,   AKRON, O.

DR. W. J. HOTTENSTEIN,

SURGEON DENTIST,

211 E. Mill Street,
Over Berry's Carpet Store,

Res. 126 Carroll St., AKRON, O.

DR. J. H. PETERSON,

106 Market Street,

AKRON, O.

BOSTON DENTAL PARLORS

DR. B. J. HILL, M'G'R,

Cor. Main and Exchange Sts.,
Over Black's Drug Store,

AKRON, O.

LAWYERS.

H. T. WILLSON,

ATTORNEY AT LAW,

109 Mill St.   Telephone 122.

AKRON, O.

W. E. YOUNG,

ATTORNEY AT LAW,

186 S. Howard St.   Opp. Post Office.

AKRON, O.

www.ingramcontent.com/pod-product-compliance
Lightning Source LLC
Chambersburg PA
CBHW030556270326
41927CB00007B/943